M000096255

For Six in Honor of Millions

Marie Peters

Seattle, WA

The memorial you see on the front cover stands outside the kitchen window of Marie's house in Montpezat. It was this memorial that inspired her research into the devastation of World War I.

© 2019 by Marie Peters

ISBN: 978-0-578-61443-4

Writing is a solo venture, but pulling everything together and creating a book takes a team. First, I wish to thank my French friends Lisette and Lorette Morant, Alain and Jakie Lafage, and Olivier Torchet, who directed me to their favorite war memorials, added historical facts about the places we visited, and faithfully encouraged me for 25 years to not give up. In the beginning my former husband Greg Terry patiently drove me on back roads in France and Australia to find war memorials. Thanks to my family and friends who never complained to my face when I repeatedly talked about "the book." To the soldiers, families, and historians who wrote and shared their experiences and knowledge of World War I. To my father, Eric Amandus Alexander Peters, who fought for the Germans as a 15-year-old merchant marine on the North Sea.

To my editor, Devon Musgrave, for his intelligence and patience in organizing the book and improving my old photos and bringing the pieces together. I'm grateful for his role as my faithful sheepdog guiding me forward when I was confused or discouraged. To Rob Nance, the illustrator and designer, whose artistic talents made the book very special for my grandchildren.

The text is set in Maiandra GD.

For all the children who became orphans during WWI and specifically
for my six grandchildren in Australia and the United States:
Shata Liam, Satchel, Fred, Charlotte, Charlie, and Cooper.
From Oma/Mamo.

And also in memory of my dear friends Lisette and Lorette.

Why I Wrote This Book

As he does every day, Michel Thrillier, a farmer in Sozieres, goes out to till his field, and doing so, he digs up his ground a little more deeply each year. His plough stumbles a bit against something. Michel discovers the remains of a human body. Next to the skeleton he brings to light a uniform, a flask, and even buckles that allow him to find out the identity of the man who wore them. Immediately the farmer goes and informs the mayor of the village and then the Commonwealth War Grave Committee situated in Arras, which is in charge of the burial places of former British Empire soldiers. Through a quick search George Russell Bassisto surfaces again.

"Down Under" some descendants are found. The family wanted to repatriate the body, but the Ministry of Defense didn't allow it. Among other reasons, it was the tradition among the British to bury the dead soldiers in a place not far from their battlefields. A few months later Bassisto was taken to a respectable grave. Draped in the Australian flag and carried by fully uniformed military people, the coffin entered the cemetery followed by bagpipes. A ceremony took place with prayers and volleys. At last the coffin with soldier Bassisto was brought down to his last resting place.

—My friend Lisette Piere Morant translated this from her local newspaper in Montpezat, France, September 1998

In a tiny hillside bastide in southwest France called Montpezat, there is a humble World War I memorial. A French soldier stoically stands and stares into the distance. Every morning and evening I see him when I open and close my shutters. Thousands of miles away an Australian soldier stands at attention in the sleepy rural town of Lancefield in Victoria. Both villages have been my home. Looking at two nearly identical statues in far distant lands fed my curiosity about WWI. Since 1994 I've photographed over 200 rural memorials in both countries. Every monument tells a different story and reflects the ideas of war, religion, politics, language, and visual arts of the time. Antiwar sympathizers, like myself, see war memorials as a statement of loss and reminders of war's horror.

About 176,000 WWI memorials stand in France. The maps in this book show where the memorials I've included are located. Just imagine how the French map would look if 176,000 memorials were represented. In Australia memorials are prominent in village and city parks, honoring the 60,000 volunteers who died and are buried in France. People walk or drive past with hardly a notice except on Armistice Day, November 11, and Anzac Day, April 25. Yet while I'm photographing memorials, an elderly person might join me and point to an engraved name. The war memories remain with the older citizens. Politicians in France and Australia attend parades and lay wreaths on national holidays, but the realities of war for most of our youth today are news reports from faraway countries, video games, drones, and superheroes.

War memorials cannot tell the stories of the 1.36 million French widows and orphans left by the war. Nor do they recognize that every second Australian family lost a relative and that returning soldiers were often handicapped by wounds and facial scars, making integration into the home society very difficult.

It is shockingly easy for me to imagine my grandchildren being forced into the same fate as the Australian soldier Bassisto. But war is totally different today and I'm not sure our youth comprehend its consequences as I did during World War II. My father had fought as a 15-year-old seaman for the Germans in WWI and he shared some of his stories. I was born in 1939 when WWII was beginning. As a child I instantly ducked when bombers flew overhead, and I feared black-outs and Japanese invasions. As a young adult I listened to the radio broadcasting body counts during the Vietnam War. In 1957 my Tante Nora warned me to be careful of unexploded bombs when I walked in the forest near Hamburg. Then 9/11 awoke the world to a new strategy of war called terrorism. War was no longer "over there."

International war remains a constant companion in modern societies. The United States maintains 800 military bases in 70 nations. North Korea is dangerously close to inflicting havoc on the world, and citizens in the Middle East experience endless conflict and destruction daily. We must increase our knowledge of war and the beliefs and trials of other countries to avoid arrogance, misconceptions, and future wars.

War memorials have not ended wars, but they can remind us and our elected leaders to continually seek cooperation between all people and countries. The consequences of war do not end with a peace treaty. The effects of war ripple down through generations and generations. I ask you:

What would our world be like today if we had used the strength, brains, leadership, and creativity of the estimated 41 million military and civilian casualties in World War I?

PART 1:
SOUTHWEST FRANCE

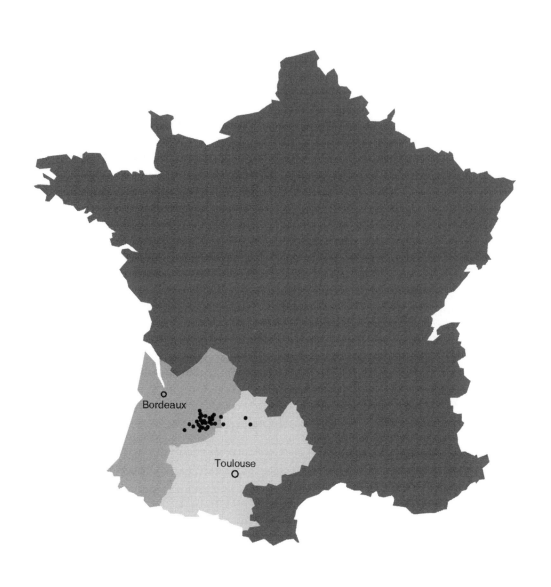

LIST OF TOWNS

Aiguillon

Aiguillon began as a Roman encampment because its site sits above the confluence of the Lot and Garonne Rivers, providing access to the two great valleys of southwest France. Today its buildings still reflect the wealth it once enjoyed although modern transportation has trivialized its strategic importance.

Aiguillon's Tuesday morning market is busy with local vendors and their customers admiring and purchasing cheese, bread, roasting chickens, fish, meats, olives, nuts, Vietnamese Yum Cha, vegetables, fruits, and practical items such as tablecloths, bedding, hats, and watches. At one table a local woman carves names into wooden napkin rings while next to her a smiling farmer wearing a black beret raises up large Marmande multicolored tomatoes. This festive market fills the central square and is the first market I visited as a new owner of a tumbledown house (formerly a blacksmithery building) in France. Because Aiguillon's weekly market is good but also for sentimental reasons, I visit it every time I return to my place in Montpezat.

Nearly 100 of Aiguillon's sons—and in at least nine cases more than one son from a single family—died during the war, and its memorial is one of the most affecting ones I've visited. A mother comforts her son with her right hand and holds a wreath in her left. It's not clear if she is looking down on a dead soldier lying beneath them or wondering where her husband is buried. Perhaps the reclining soldier represents the thousands of lost soldiers now buried somewhere far from their families and villages. It is both dramatic and deeply sad. Given its mood, it is appropriately located in its own small square before the church, rather than in the middle of the market square. Through the years the monument has been well cared for, and on my last visit several healthy red roses were blooming.

WWI 94 killed
2 Sailhan
2 Vincent
2 Bouchon
2 Brassier
2 Dubroca
2 Dulin
2 Dupony
2 Lompech
2 Lamothe
WWII 20
Algiers 19
Franco-Prussian 12

Armillac

North of the Lot and Garonne Rivers near the town of Seyches, you begin to see the unique wrought-iron crosses that are typical of the region. Most of the crosses have dates from the 1800s, and I've been told they were probably religious monuments. These intricately designed crosses are also placed on top of the war memorials in this area. East of Seyches on Route 667, Armillac is a tiny town with a magnificent view and a small medieval church. The cross that tops its World War I memorial is decorated with the symbols of the village tradesmen and a sword and arrow. A Madonna sits in the centermost part of the cross. It took some time to find the memorial because it sits near the back of the church.

As with most of the towns in the Lot-et-Garonne district, Armillac is devoted to farming. In summer the rolling fields are covered in sunflowers, grain, and corn. There are very few houses in the village, so it was shocking to read that this miniscule hamlet lost twelve people in the war.

WWI 12
WWII 0

Bias

Bias is a small, quiet town along the Lot River. It is also the town where I made a big mistake about the WWI war memorial. On my first visit I passed a grand 14th-century Romanesque church and saw a very beautiful wall niche that held a large marble statue of either the Madonna or Mother France, holding a fallen victim of the war. A bouquet of porcelain flowers was tucked into the soldier's hands and a bouquet of real flowers stood at the base. The center of the memorial simply states, "Anciens Combattents De Bias." I assumed this was the Bias WWI war memorial.

Five years ago, I revisited the Bias memorial but continued driving through the village in search of the indoor swimming pool. I never found the pool, but I discovered another magnificent WWI war memorial situated beside the cemetery. A tall and proud winged Marianne, the mother of France, stands at the top of a three-tiered monument. She holds the war helmet of a fallen soldier in her right hand and an olive branch in her left hand. Her long hair and graceful robe flow around her body. She stands on the top tier, which is decorated with a crown and branches and the words "Aux Enfants De Bias Morts Pour La France." Lion heads with closed eyes add to the overall feelings of anguish. On each side of the memorial are small relief depictions of war. The first one shows a soldier in uniform saying goodbye to his wife and child. The second relief shows a soldier in the trenches preparing to throw a hand grenade. In the third relief an angel comforts the wife. The final relief places the wife and child under a leafless tree holding one another in silent sorrow.

The quiet private setting of the Bias memorial—a wall of green cypress trees behind the white statue, a bright blue sky outlining the beautiful statue of Marianne, and the touching story that depicts the reality of those left behind—make this memorial one of my favorites. Bias suffered heavily in WWI. Seven sons died in 1914, three in 1915, four in 1916, six in 1917, five in 1918, and one in 1919.

| WWI 26 |
| WWII 3 |

Everything, everything in war is barbaric.... But the worst barbarity of war is that it forces men collectively to commit acts against which individually they would revolt with their whole being.

—Ellen Key, *War, Peace, and the Future* (1916)

Casseneiul

For centuries the ancient town of Casseneuil has occupied the peninsula created by the Lot and Lède Rivers. Originally the town depended on river transport and trade for its wealth. It held out against the English during the Hundred Years' War (1337–1453) and was frequently plundered by enemies. Over the last twenty years the town has consistently preserved the oldest parts of the village and maintained the footprints of the original buildings. It is a beautiful, medieval walled town, flanked by the Lot River to the south while the Lède River surrounds the town and provides a pastoral walk for villagers and visitors. The bridge over the Sône River, which joins the Lède at the north end of the peninsula, is a good spot for fishing. On many visits I've rested along the river and watched fishermen gazing at their lines in the still water, but I've never seen anyone catch a fish.

In the town you can admire old gracious half-timbered houses, many flanking the rivers, parks, and narrow crooked streets meandering through the oldest section of Casseneuil. Take a slow wander to the archeological sites and riverside park for a rest at one of the picnic tables. During summer you can hire a rental boat on the Lot and or play water volleyball on the Lède.

The war memorial must be large to hold the fifty names of the fallen soldiers from the area. The decoration is a pair of stylized swords on both sides of the names. A high green hedge rises behind the wall of the cemetery and across the street is the river park. In my opinion the war memorial could be better positioned. It does not offer the space for contemplation due to the busy road in front of the memorial. However, if you brave the traffic to read the names of villagers engraved on the memorial and note that three families lost two family members each, you will once again be touched by the massive destruction caused by war.

```
WWI 50
WWII 17
```

11

August 4, 1914: Invasion of Belgium

When German soldiers were pushed to reach Paris through Belgium, their commanders ordered them to break international norms of war by killing civilians, burning houses and barns, and stealing and ruining food sources. The strategic plan was to reach Paris as soon as possible. Priests were singled out for torture and death. Tens of thousands of soldiers from both sides were killed and wounded. Civilians became refugees without support, shelter, and food. After the war ended, many civilian bodies were found in common graves along the German path through Belgium. It is now an accepted fact that more civilians were killed than soldiers during the invasion of Belgium. Civilians in all countries died from executions, burning and demolished buildings, artillery fire, bombs, starvation, displacement, exposure, stress, and anguish. In 1916, relief organizations estimated that as many as 200,000 children were already orphaned or left with one parent in France.

Burial of Germans (Langemark Cemetery)

In 2018, I traveled with my teenage grandsons to Belgium and France to learn about WWI. Most history scholars advise you to study WWI in order to understand WWII. I wanted to learn about it because of my German family and my project to write about WWI war memorials in France and Australia.

Beginning in January 1915, cemeteries were made for thousands of dead soldiers. In the beginning the bodies were buried quickly and near where they fell, but eventually those bodies had to be put in a cemetery. Imagine how emotionally difficult it must have been for French civilians to prepare the graves and bury German soldiers. Langemark is a German cemetery on French soil, and it has a very different mood from the Allied cemeteries with their rows and rows of white crosses or headstones. The German crosses are made of dark gray metal with rounded edges and tall somber pine trees were planted amongst the graves. Under each cross five to seven German soldiers are buried upon each other with name indications on plaques. But most bodies of WWI soldiers were blown apart in battle, making identification impossible. The bones and body parts of 25,000 German soldiers are in a mass grave.

We, like other visitors, wandered quietly around the cemetery, trying to comprehend that 25,000 unknown young German men lie together in a grave or on top of each other under the metal crosses. It was a deeply emotional experience

Casteljaloux

Casteljaloux is situated on the edge of the Landes pine forests, formerly a hunting preserve of the important D'Alberts and of Henri IV. The French automatically think of this area as the base of the Cadets de Gascogne in *Cyrano de Bergerac*. "Casteljaloux" sounds like the French word for "jealous"—"jaloux"—but actually comes from "gelos," or perilous. The town center has a good number of half-timbered, corbelled houses built in the fifteenth and sixteenth centuries, when the town was the capital of Gascony and a base for Henri IV's hunting adventures. At the end of town are the Bains de Casteljaloux with their pools, sauna, boating, and beaches. The pretty beaches bordering Lac de Clarens is another popular vacation spot.

It was a moody spring day when I photographed the war memorial, and magically the sun hid under a large grey cloud, providing a magnificent background for the statue. A large bouquet of red, white, and blue flowers decorated the site. An older and more modest war memorial stood on the side. Seventy-six sons who died in World War I are remembered on the older plaque. I couldn't find a list of those who died in World War II.

This monument is a favorite of mine because it was very easy to imagine the bleak loneliness the young men must have felt while waiting in the cold wet trenches day in and day out.

WWI 76
WWII ?

14

1914 — 1918

AGUT Paul	DESPIN Henri
ARANDA Joseph	DESTRAC Elie
ARANDA Louis	DOUX Georges
ARCHÉ Paul	DUBERNET Pierre
ARNAUD Jules	DUBOIS Georges
AUGÉ Raymond	DUBOURG Gaston
BARÉNOT Jacques	DUBOURG André
BAREYRE Pierre	DUCAS Gaston
BAREYRE Joseph	DUHURT Marcel
BAZAS Fernand	DUMERC Marcel
BAZIN Isidore	DUPRAT Roger
BERNÈDE Pierre	DUTREIL-LASSUS
BERTRIN Jean	ESCOUBET Jean
BOISSONNOT Calé	FERRAND Jean
BONNET Fernand	FRÈCHE Pierre
BOUCHET Jules	GAILLÈRES Bernᴰ
BOUCHON Eugène	GAJAC Henri
BOUISSON Blaise	GARBAY Louis
BROTHIER Maurice	GARRIGUES Moïse
BROUCH Jacques	GASPALOU Pierre
CAMPAGNE Marcel	GAUBE Jean
CANOT Jean	GAUBE Jean
CANTEGRIT Louis	GAUBE Clément
CANTILLAC Jean	CERMA Joseph
CAPES Jean	GISCOS Jean
CAPES Julien	GODARD André
CARDOIT Julien	GODARD Pierre
CARDOUAT Jean	GOURGUES Pierre
CAZENAVE Albᵗ	GUILHEM Etienne
COL André	GUIONNET Marcel
COURSAN Jules	GUITARD Pierre
COURSAN Léon	HIOLLET Jean
COUSINET Jean	JOURDAN Albert
DANEY Louis	JOURDAN Léopᵈ
DARROUMAN Jean	LABADIE Jean
DAUDIGEOS Louis	LABADIE Louis
LAURTIEU Georges	LABAN Gaston
...ENOT Georges	BLANCHARD Eloi

16

Most war memorials, which stand in schools and churchyards all over Europe, whether they portray solemn soldiers, mourning families, or merely list names of the fallen, insist that those who died in the war did not die in vain.

—Niall Ferguson, *The Pity of War* (1999)

Castelmoron-sur-Lot

The nicest way to enter this village is over a handsome bridge that crosses the Lot River. Traditional buildings with red tile roofs and fanciful turrets flank the river. A small path runs beneath the buildings and alongside the slow-moving river as it twists and turns through the gentle hills covered with groomed forests, vineyards, and orchards.

The village center has a large covered courtyard and a grandiose fountain sits in the middle of the town square. It is painted in a pale robin's-egg blue that matches the many benches of the same color. Across the street another plaza is in front of the church and more blue benches offer a place to rest. Shade comes from old gnarled plane trees pruned into foreboding shapes. A swimming beach with rental boats is across the river from the beautiful Moorish-style town hall. The weekly outdoor market is a friendly place to do your shopping on Wednesdays. It is a busy village with all the conveniences, including two excellent bakeries.

The war memorial is not in the town square or plaza. It is further down the main road nestled into a tall, green hedge. A beautifully carved mother of France stands on the pedestal, and the names of the fallen men are carved on a large plaque beneath the statue. In spring and summer fresh pansies bounce gaily in large urns.

Across the street men play boules in another park. Today they watch me with curiosity. As I copy the victims' names and search for the name of the monument's architect, a man wearing a black beret comes over and points to the name Chaumont. He then points to himself and shakes his right hand in the traditionally southwest French manner, which means either very good or very bad. He grins a broken-tooth smile, offers his hand, and, with a tiny bow, returns to the game. The two Chaumont boys are still remembered by this old man.

WWI 52
2 Cazautet
2 Chaumont
2 Costes
2 Couton
WWII 3

Shata Liam

Clairac

Lisette, a dear French friend, wanted me to see this memorial because she thought it was an especially lovely motif that reminded her of the many years she taught children and adults.

Clairac was once a Protestant town. Besieged by Louis XIII in 1621, its fortifications were razed. However, about fifteen half-timbered houses survive. The town's Benedictine abbey was founded in the seventh century, and by the thirteenth century it was the most influential abbey in the Agenais region. Now it is closed to the public because it is privately owned. The timbered Maison Montesquieu is where the writer of the same name is believed to have written his famous political satire, *Persian Letters*, in 1721.

The World War I memorial is in a beautiful park near the *mairie* (town hall). A rounded wall behind the statue displays the names of the fallen etched on white stone slabs. Two steps up take you to a mosaic floor and a bench. One hundred and seven men from Clairac are commemorated. The statue shows a beautiful woman encouraging a young boy to comprehend a powerful message. She might symbolize Mother France, but I think she represents the many mothers widowed by the war. Her dress is made of simple material and she wears wooden shoes. With one arm she draws the child close to her, and he places an arm on her shoulder. The statue captures a tender moment between an adult and child. Could she be telling him about his father or warning him about the sorrow of war? On her lap she holds a large open book with the words "Livre d' Or de la Grande Guerre."

Each year on November 11 the memorial is decorated with numerous French flags, potted plants, and red, white, and blue fresh flower bouquets. Over the years I've visited this memorial many times, and often there were smaller bouquets left at the base of the statue. Sometimes a name was attached to a bouquet. The citizens of Clairac remember their fallen sons. Ten families lost two sons each.

WWI 107 killed
WWII 25 killed
Indochin 1 killed
Deporte 1 killed
Algerie 2 killed

Calm fell. From Heaven distilled a clemency;
There was peace on earth, and silence in the sky;
Some could, some could not, shake off misery:
The Sinister Spirit sneered: 'It had to be!'
And again the Spirit of Pity whispered, 'Why?'

—Thomas Hardy, "And There Was a Great Calm" (1918)

Clermont-Dessous

Wandering through the hills and valleys on my way toward Port-Saint-Marie, I happened upon the tiny, well cared for, and extremely charming village of Clermont-Dessous. A curvy road takes you to a hill-top overlooking the Garonne River. The parking lot is below the village, but after a short and easy walk up the small hill and past the stone church you'll arrive at a view point. Far below you'll see the train tracks along the wide and strong Garonne and beyond the river fertile orchards and farm land. The cemetery sits below the church.

Take time to enter the church and enjoy the cool air and serene atmosphere. Gradually your eyes will adjust to the light and you'll see a war memorial hanging on the church wall. Most churches have war memorials commemorating the congregation's fallen soldiers. Village or commune war memorials are usually erected in the town or in a park. All names of the local soldiers who served in the war are honored on those war memorials. But you won't find the commune war memorial in Clermont-Dessous. It stands proudly along the river bank in a simple park large enough for people to pay homage to all the fallen sons of the commune.

Before you leave Clermont-Dessous, walk up the tiny street and enjoy the enticing collection of homes and cafes. Don't pass up the opportunity to sit under the green trees sipping a cup of tea and savoring a crepe at one of the restaurants.

When you arrive at the commune war memorial along the river, you'll see a fifty-year anniversary plaque at its base. On each side of the monument are beautiful carvings, bronze wreaths, and branches. A sad mother of France stands at an angle, roses in her hand, which she appears to be dropping onto the bouquet of roses carved at the base. In her left hand she might be clutching a broken sword.

WWI 20 killed
WWII 3 killed

1914 1918

LA PAROISSE
DE CLERMONT-DESSOUS
A SES ENFANTS
MORTS POUR LA FRANCE

CAUBOUE Léo 28 Août 1914
MONTEILS Roger 20 Xbre ....
DUBROCA Roger 17 Fer 1915
ESCOUBET Jean 19 9bre ....
MALLIÉ Jean 27 Avril 1916
LAFFAGE Léonce 11 Mai ....
JARDEL Justin 9 Juin ....
TARNAC Eloi 9 Janvier 1919
BARTHE Jean 26 Janvier ....

REQUIEM ÆTERNAM DONA EIS DOMINE

28

War was a baptism for most World War I soldiers; an unforgettable initiation into a murderous folly which spurred them on to kill, to go on killing, faster and faster, speeding up the firing rate, pushing it to the furthest limit of endurance for both guns and men. It transformed them from peaceable chaps hardly capable of killing a hen into a species of happy barbarians who shouted for joy when their shrapnel burst among the cavalry or infantry or, best of all, in the middle of the enemy gun emplacement. The enemy surrounded them with missiles, launched its red and black scrolls into the sky; as the ammunition spun away and exploded, it tossed pieces of shredded corpse all around.

—Words from a soldier in the 5th Artillery Regiment under Colonel Neville and part of the 7th Army Corps of General Dubail's 1st Army, assigned to the Army of Alsace under General Pau.

Coulx

Driving north from Castelmoron-sur-Lot for about six miles, you will see a small road heading west. Take this narrow road through rolling fields of traditional crops like sunflowers, corn, grape vines, and orchards of plum trees. The plums will become the famous prunes d'Agen. These high-quality plums have been harvested in small farms throughout the Lot-et-Garonne area since the Middle Ages when monks returned from the Crusades with plum seeds. If you want to sample an Agen prune, just go to the famous Fran's Chocolates store in Seattle and ask for the delicious prunes that are imported from France and then dipped in rich dark chocolate. You'll discover that an Agen prune is something very different from the typical dried prune found in the U.S.

Coulx is tiny. It consists of the mairie, the church with a two-bell tower but only one bell, barns, a sports field, and graveyard. There is a fine restored windmill on the top of a nearby hill. In case you can't find Coulx on your map, it is located between Tombebœuf and Castelmoron-sur-Lot, a little closer to Tombebœuf.

The two times I visited this memorial I was surprised to see people gathered around the mairie. Once I enjoyed watching a group of happy teenagers having a party in the attached common center of the mairie, and another time I watched five laughing women entering the mairie. Most country villages are very quiet, and I often wonder if anyone lives there. Coulx is not more than a hamlet but seems to be a thriving little village. Seeing the small groups of local citizens enjoying the facilities of their mairie made me very happy. On the other hand, when I surveyed the small collection of buildings, I became overcome with sorrow. It was difficult to imagine that eighteen young men of tiny Coulx were killed in the First World War.

> WWI 17 killed plus 1 more died later from wounds
> WWII 1 killed in Tunisia

Cours

When first I saw the memorial at Cours, I thought the rifle the soldier was holding was real because of its realistic colors. But it is merely an excellent copy, cleverly painted.

Cours is a tiny village on a loop in the road between Dolmayrac and Laugnac about half-way between the Lot and Garonne Rivers in the Lot-et-Garonne department. Like all of its neighbors, it is situated on top of a small hill with rolling farmland all around. At its center stands the small church. Oriented as so many are along an east-west axis with the door to the west and the altar to the east, the church has a slightly derelict air and our arrival caused many pigeons to take flight. On the west side of the church stands a massive barn, the sort used to shelter the herd in winter. On the east side stands the memorial.

Shaded by the church in the evening sun, the memorial stands in a small stone square with heavy chain ropes around it. A small bench beneath an old tree welcomes those who wish to pause and remember. For years an old brown dog would wander to me for a little attention. It was a sad day for me when he no longer came for a gentle pat on the head.

WWI 12 killed

Damazan

Damazan is situated on a small canal west of Aiguillon and east of Casteljaloux, much closer to Aiguillon. Boating, kayaking, sail boarding, swimming, and picnicking are some of the tourist attractions. In April, the canal was full of weekenders enjoying the water and relaxing.

Inside the village you'll find cream-colored houses with a variety of brightly colored shutters. Half-timbered houses add to the alluring courtyard and the small stone-covered streets. The town hall is built over the covered village market square, which provides a warm and dry place for vendors and shoppers.

The war memorial stands in a nearby park surrounded by numerous boules courts. Several teams were playing when I arrived. They respectfully watched me photograph the war memorial. and when I left they returned to their game. The war memorial is large and features a beautiful but pensive young woman sitting at the base of the memorial gazing upon the names of the fallen. She most likely represents the Mother of France, but again it is very easy to imagine her as a sorrowful widow. Over 66 soldiers fell in Marne, Yser, Flandres, Artois, Somme, Aisne, and Champagne.

WWI Over 66 fallen
WWII 4 fallen

Two hundred years will not suffice to erase the traces of this tragedy.

—Harron Parry, English soldier, dead at 20 (1917)

Dausse

Dausse is a typical small village on the road between two beautiful towns in France: Penne-d'Agenais and Tournon-d'Agenais. Its modest memorial sits in front of a yellow stone church along the roadside, commemorating the death of twelve of its citizens, four of whom, it notes, were noncommissioned officers. The memorial was the only one of its sort we saw: a cylinder pedestal with a painted top and a wreath and palm frond running around it. This photo was taken in the summer, when the many boules players are thankful for the plane trees' large shady branches.

The nineteenth-century French novelist Stendhal compared the rolling hills and valleys of this area to Tuscany. Its fertile land produces every kind of fruit and vegetables and is often called the orchard of Europe. Many small vineyards produce wines that compare favorably with Bordeaux, Bergerac, and Cahors, but with lower price tags.

The Lot-et-Garonne region is familiar with war. Once held by the kings of France, the kings of England, and the dukes of Aquitaine, it endured bitter disputes in the fourteenth and fifteenth centuries, otherwise called the Hundred Years' War. In the late 1400s the English gradually gave up their territories, but many English traditions persist in the area. For example, rugby remains a very popular sport in Lot-et-Garonne.

WWI 12

A Trip to Douaumont Fort

As we arrived at Fort de Douaumont, our guide informed us that a German soldier's body was discovered two weeks earlier by workers enlarging the parking lot. The boys were amazed and asked if that happens often. He said "Yes, parts of bodies or debris from war are still found in fields or woods." We were aware of that after visiting a farm in Belgium where the farmer collected objects found in his fields. The many shells and other objects were displayed on tables, floor, and the walls, including an Australian flag and a shoe with a toe bone still inside it. Now farmers put special protection on their tractors in case they might hit an unexploded bomb or shell. They call these items the IRON CROP. The guide encouraged the kids to hunt for war items in the surrounding woods. After ten minutes, each teenager returned with at least one war item: a button, piece of leather, and several shells. They also experienced the clay mud that soldiers hated. Their shoes were caked in heavy mud that was next to impossible to remove.

Fort Douaumont was hit heavily by the Germans, but with some renovation it is in re-markably good shape, considering the months of pounding it took by the Germans. We wandered through the gloomy damp corridors where bats flew overhead, saw the soldiers' beds, larger rooms for meals, narrow winding stairs, a small chapel for prayer, and the retractable turret for a 155mm gun. It was easy to imagine the fear and stress the soldiers endured by constant German bombarding. Then the guide took us to a point where he could reproduce the noise of one shell hitting the fort. The noise made me automatically duck and cover my ears. It was a huge thumping noise that felt like it was shaking my internal body. The guide asked us to imagine what it would have been like to endure that noise hour after hour, day after day. That evening we discussed battle fatigue and stress with a greater understanding. The last stop was a walled-up gallery that contained the remnants of several dozen soldiers killed during the battles.

New War Strategies #1

HELMETS: During the first 18 months of the war, the soldiers wore cloth hats and many deaths might have been prevented with metal hats. The first metal helmets were not designed to protect the ears. A Howitzer 155 makes a very loud noise and many soldiers suffered from hearing problems.

HORSES: The horse was no longer a charging mount for WWI because war strategies had changed. The horse primarily was a beast of burden, pulling wagons, artillery pieces, and ambulances and racing messages to the front. One million horses were used in WWI and only 62,000 returned. The horses were needed, but they consumed tons and tons more food than for soldiers.

Fumel

Fumel is a large town on the Lot River. At first sight it is busy and industrial, but when you climb up towards the Centre Ville its character changes as old buildings become more common. The old town is on the hillside on the north bank of the Lot.

The war memorial here is in a large square, which serves primarily as a children's park with play equipment and other attractions. The memorial forms one end of the park with a long low wall with two statues. One statue is to commemorate those lost in the Franco-Prussian War of 1870–71; the statue shown here commemorates the First World War. They are linked by a pond and a trickling fountain.

The statue itself appears to be an angel or the god Mars, holding a fallen soldier who lies across a cannon. The sculptor was Jean Magron. Beneath the sculpture is DeGaulle's June 1940 exhortation from London to his countrymen, urging them to ensure that France does not die. Set in the wall is a small tribute to the widows and orphans who were also victims of the war. Eighty-four names grace the memorial, including several with the same surname, suggesting families who lost two or three sons.

WWI 84
2 Maury
2 Bord
2 Carles
2 Delord
2 Escande
3 Delrieu

Galapian

Galapian sits on a ridge between the Garonne and the Lot Rivers near their confluence, just east of the small town of Lagarrigue, which is east of Aiguillon. In small villages like this one you rarely see people on the streets and the shutters are often closed, either because the residents are away or they're taking their midday nap. But you can see beautiful views of a rich countryside in every direction. The town itself is small and typical of many in Lot-et-Garrone. In winter the pale blue shutters add color, as do the remaining red apples on the leafless trees.

The war memorial stands proudly in front of the mairie and alongside a narrow medieval arch, where birds find cozy spaces for their nests.

The soldier is distinctive due to the detailed painting of his shoes, uniform, war equipment, and his prominent mustache. The stone base is relatively large, considering that only eleven names are engraved on it. Six more names were added after World War II and one more after the Vietnam War. The location of the statue and its detailed painting make this war memorial unique.

WWI	11
WWII	6
Vietnam	1

Satchel

Granges-sur-Lot

The Lot River has been a major thoroughfare from ancient times. The Romans knew it well, the Crusaders followed its course, and the English in the Middle Ages sourced their wine from Cahors along its banks. Over the course of history many beautiful towns and villages were built along its banks to take advantage of its great beauty.

Unfortunately, Granges-sur-Lot is no longer a dynamic village. Although it is situated along the river's banks, the river in that area flows along a wide flat plain to the south and Granges is on the south side. The village boasts a very pretty town square surrounded by the eighteenth-century buildings, but it doesn't have the views of the river characteristic of its neighbors built on the steeper banks along other sections of the river.

Like Montpezat and Laugnac, Granges has a secular location for its war memorial, in the center of the town square. It commemorates the death of fifteen inhabitants in World War I and, as is so typical in this part of France, only one in World War II. The memorial is a large white pedestal with the proud Gallic rooster, an unofficial national symbol of France, at its summit. It's interesting that even among educated French, the significance of the rooster ("coq" in French) as a symbol of France is not well understood, but I was told by our local doctor, Alain Lafage, that "Gallia," the Roman name for France, comes from the Latin word for rooster, "gallus."

To the west of town are new sport fields for soccer and rugby, a sign that this was English territory before the Hundred Years' War. It is also home of a flourishing plum orchard. Tourists can visit the orchard and a museum that features an interesting film covering the history of plums, and in August my grandsons and I watched the harvest. After learning about the farming of the plums, you can walk through a seriously complicated corn maze or you can stay in the gift shop and tempt yourself with many plum delicacies and ice cream.

WWI 15

Houeillès

Houeillès is south of Casteljaloux, past Pompogne, and is a fairly large town for southwest France. I didn't get to explore much of it because the light was growing weak, but the war memorial was easy to find because it sits beside the main thoroughfare of the town. It appears to be relatively new. Many memorials were refurbished or replaced for the hundredth anniversary of the Great War.

This memorial is a simple obelisk made of dark gray granite. A decoration on the side appears to be a tree of life. Below is a darker plaque listing the twelve names of the town's fallen sons. Obelisks were often used for war memorials, representing strength, endurance, and courage.

Near the memorial three neighbors were visiting and seemed very curious about what I was doing. While I took photographs, an elderly lady crossed the street and greeted me with a friendly smile. She pointed to the name "Brignolles, Arnaud" and then toward herself.

I assumed she was a relative. It's at times like this that I become very embarrassed that I can't speak French. I told her "I am an American." She gave me an even bigger smile and then a brief French hug and air kiss on each cheek. I pointed to my eyes and acted sad with tears running down my cheeks. She quickly said, "Oui, oui." As she crossed the street again, I turned around for a last look at Arnaud's name. The tall flag poles stood proud, strong, and ready to fly the French tricolor flag. In the background was the Houeillès mairie standing guard. Arnaud Brignolles is remembered.

A LA
MÉMOIRE GLORIEUSE
DES ENFANTS DE
HOUEILLES
MORTS POUR LA FRANCE
1914 — 1918

Lacépède

Like many villages in southwest France, Lacépède sits on a hilltop above the Lot River; it is not far from the confluence with the Garonne River. This memorial is interesting because if you stand directly in front of it, it appears as if the large cemetery crucifix behind the statue is actually an extension of the war memorial.

On closer inspection you see the war memorial stands alone on a platform with bomb-shell cartridges positioned on each corner. It's my understanding that these are war trophies and reminders of the horror and hatefulness of war. Alongside the memorial four large cypress trees stand at attention as if guarding the twenty-five fallen soldiers.

The war memorial is not crowded in a small space near the mairie or church or along a roadside. This memorial is placed prominently in the cemetery with gravel walking trails leading to it. You feel as if you are in a park rather than a cemetery. If a bench were provided, it would be a pleasant spot to sit and absorb the magnitude of what these soldiers defended and to offer your heartfelt gratitude for their efforts.

The white pillar is decorated with palm branches and a resting helmet with olive branches. One black plaque visibly declares honor to "AUX ENFANTS, de LACEPEDE MORTS pour la FRANCE 1914-1918." The lower black plaques on the front and sides of the pillar list the names of the dead.

The peacefulness of the site and the beautiful view over the rolling hills and green farmlands are perfect for personal reflection. An ancient stone fence covered with green moss, ivy, and lilac blossoms contributes to this beautiful war memorial and where it stands.

WWI 25

Laugnac

Compared to many of the villages described in this book, Laugnac was a veritable metropolis. In addition to the traditional alimentaire and boulangerie, it had a hotel restaurant and a bar restaurant. It is situated on route D13 between Agen and Castelmoron-sur-Lot but succeeds in turning its back on the traffic along that road by having the road skirt along the western edge of the town. At the center of the town is the town square, which is a small park with lawns and large trees. And near the center of the park is the war memorial. Now it is a more tranquil, quiet village.

Some war memorials are downcast, the soldiers stooped, the rifle muzzle down to the ground. Not so at Laugnac. Here an almost jaunty soldier with a luxuriant mustache holds his head up and his rifle as it should be, muzzle upward and ready for action. The pedestal on which he stands is surrounded by a square low fence with a little gate to permit entry and two large bombshells flanking it on either side.

From where he stands the soldier can watch the boules players and can see the hunters arrive at the bars for sustenance after a day of the chase. He can also watch the dwindling generations of children play in the park as they grow up in the free France that he helped secure. Few, if any, look up at him anymore, and all are surprised that a strange woman has stopped in the town to photograph the memorial and note down the particulars. But if the young are disappearing to the cities, the names on the pedestal remain the names of the aging farmers and retired folk who stroll gently to the bars as night falls to take their aperitifs and discuss the rugby. These descendants still mark November 11 with a special ceremony at the memorial. More often than that, no doubt, they still remember their ancestors who did not return.

WWI 21 killed, listed according to the year they died

54

Le Lédat

Le Lédat is not a village you pass through—it is between Villeneuve-sur-Lot and Casseneuil but north of the road that connects the two. Nor is it a village you would normally visit as a destination, lacking any sites of major historical interest. But those who do chance upon Le Lédat are rewarded in several ways.

First, because the village has the charm typical of the area, with old stone buildings clustered around a substantial church. Also, because Le Lédat had an excellent restaurant popular with the cognoscenti of the surrounding area. Sadly, the chef moved to Paris. Finally, because as you weave into the village along a narrow road between buildings, you turn a bend and there before you is the war memorial framed by manicured trees and with the church steeple as the backdrop immediately behind.

The memorial itself is a pedestal distinguished from the many others in this area only by the two crossed flags painted on the front. It commemorates the loss of twenty-four citizens—a staggering body count for a village of this size.

WWI 24

Le Temple-sur-Lot

Le Temple-sur-Lot is famous for a fourteenth-century building that was one of many headquarters of the Knights Templar. It has been partially restored and now acts as a conference center and sport complex. The Templars were a religious and military order founded in 1119. They supported and protected pilgrims in the Holy Land and adopted the Rules of St. Benedict. As gifts and donations of property flowed to them from pilgrims and crusaders, they became bankers to kings, popes, and merchants. By the thirteenth century, they owned more than 9,000 fortresses in the Holy Land, Malta, and France. Gradually, they grew very rich and lost sight of their original mission. At the same time, King Philip IV needed to grow his revenue. To everyone's shock, the Templars in France were arrested and their property confiscated. The king's charge was that they lost the Holy Land. Between 1307 and 1314, most Templars were imprisoned, tortured, and burned at the stake. Just before the Grand Master of the Knights Templar died, he cursed the king and pope, saying they would be dead within a year. Both king and pope died within the year.

Behind the village is the beautiful Latour Marliac Jardin des Nenuphars, an impressive and peaceful nursery with a small museum, gift shop, and cafe. Two hundred types of water lilies, many in the original handmade pots especially designed for them, make for a unique sight. This was the first French nursery to grow colored water lilies. After a visit to the nursery, Claude Monet purchased the now famous water lilies featured in his paintings of his Giverny garden.

The war memorial is very dramatic, even harrowing. It sits in front of a newly built town square with a large rectangular pond and fountain. The statue depicts a soldier in the moment of being shot. He clutches a flag, his knees are buckling, and his facial expression is one of total shock. In his right hand he holds a grenade as if he were about to toss it. A smaller monument, probably the original one, is in front, listing twenty-six names. An almost identical statue of a falling soldier is found on the memorials of Tournon-d'Agenais and Tombebœuf.

WWI 26 killed
WWII 0 killed
Algeria 2 killed

Madaillan

Roaming through the countryside I noticed an imposing chateau on a nearby hill. Suddenly a large flock of pigeons resting in the bare tree branches took flight. Surprised by the number of birds, I thought to myself, "This farm needs a dovecote." Later I learned the impressive building was Le Château Féodal de Madaillan.

Continuing along the curvy road, I spotted a large sand-covered space that might have a monument. As I parked the car, the traditional bomb casings at the four corners of the display came into view. I drew closer and bronze pineapples placed on top of the casings surprised me; these were a significant departure from usual war memorials. When my eyes rose to the dignified bronze warrior, my heart jumped. He was placed in a pose similar to the classic pose for Rodin's The Thinker but dressed in Roman attire. His head rested on his fist while he sat contemplating the meaning of war. How did this very unique statue come to be along the road, and who placed it here? Perhaps the statue represents a son from the grand chateau and it was commissioned by the landowner. If that is the case, then the benefactor honored all 23 men from the Madaillan area. The bronze gleamed in the afternoon sun and I couldn't stop pondering the meaning behind this beautiful and unique war memorial.

Years later, Devon Musgrave, editor of this book, joined me in France to take digital photos of the French war memorials. Enjoying the beautiful countryside, I assumed we had simply missed the dramatic bronze figure originally situated beside a quiet road. After a few more drives around the village, we parked near a new war memorial across the street from the mairie or town counsel office. Still very confused, I climbed the stairs next to a nursery school and waited outside the mayor's office. After she finished a telephone conversation, she graciously invited me to sit down at her desk. All was very formal, and once again I chastised myself for not speaking French. I opened the draft of the book and pointed to the original bronze statue. Her face grew very sad, and she slowly shook her head back and forth. She explained the beautiful war memorial had been stolen. I instinctively grasped her hands in mutual compassion. She described her dismay the morning she discovered the war memorial was gone; she said that the police never found the robbers. Very politely, she asked to see the photo. She skimmed through the other pages before passing the draft back to me. I promised to bring her a copy of the finished book.

> WWI 23 killed
>
> WWII 3 killed
>
> Franco-Prussian War of 1870 5 killed

What I need is hope. When we were in Artois, I lost heart to see all those dead bodies, the horrible wounds, and the butchery of Notre-Dame-de-Larette and Viony, across from Lens. Poor Frenchmen, poor Moroccans, poor Boches. They tossed them into carts, one after another, as though they had never been anything at all. One time there was a fat fellow up in a cart packing in the corpses, arranging them so they would take the least amount of space as he walked all over them.

—Sebastian Japrisot, *A Very Long Engagement* (1993)

Monclar d'Agenais

Monclar d'Agenais is a bastide perched on a narrow spit of land not far from my house in Montpezat d'Agenais but on the north side of the Lot River. Like Monflanquin, this bastide was established by Alphonse of Poitiers. After driving through rolling hills and rich farmland, you'll begin a slow climb to the town center. Quickly you'll be in front of the elegant white mairie and this grand war memorial.

A proud lady with tall spreading wings wears a helmet and holds a palm branch in one hand and a wreath in the other. This must be Mother France, otherwise known as Marianne. On my first visit several years ago, both wings were broken, but they have since been repaired and the entire monument has been scrubbed clean. On top of the memorial is a cross, and colorful pansies add color around the base. The memorial is beautiful in its grandeur and as a symbol of French pride and love of country. A plaque lists all the fallen from "Le commune de Monclar d'Agenais A Ses Infants Morts au Champ D'Honneux. 1914-1918." The architect was Gaston Rapin.

From its elevated situation the town offers magnificent views of the Tolzac valley. One side of the town's main square is lined with graceful arcades. The covered market abuts the Saint-Clar church, which has a sixteenth-century porch. If you have time, visit the church, light a candle, and ponder the larger questions of war.

WWI 44 killed

Monflanquin

North of the Lot River, Monflanquin is officially designated as one of the most beautiful villages in France. It follows the shape of the hilltop in an oval plan, and parts of the town seem to cling to the hillside that rises sharply from the valley below. Alphonse de Poitiers acquired the "mountain of Monflanquin" in 1252, and the bastide received its charter in 1256. It was an English bastide but on the border to French land, which explains its ramparts and towers. Like the fate of so many towns of southwest France, the rulers changed with the winds of war. After the Hundred Years' War, it was returned to the French. During the French Wars of Religion (1562–98), Monflanquin was a Protestant town and its fortifications played a part during the Reformation and Catholic attacks. It was recognized as a Protestant place of safety in 1598. Louis XIII dismantled the ramparts and now the surrounding boulevard uses the space.

The streets intersect at the center of town at the top of the hill with a magnificent square surrounded by arcaded houses. This square is always depicted as the model for the architecture of the region, and the town includes a good museum describing the history of Monflanquin and of bastides in general. The square had no room for recent additions like war memorials, so the glorious children who fell for France—to quote the memorial—are not commemorated within the town but rather on its edge in a beautifully maintained garden of forget-me-nots and other flowers. It depicts a soldier holding the wreath of victory aloft in his right hand and a rifle in the at-ease position in his left. No names are listed here, but the care with which the garden is kept tells us that the names are not forgotten.

East a short distance is the great fortified castle of Bonaguil. T.E. Lawrence wrote to his mother in 1908, "It is so perfect that it is almost ridiculous to call it a ruin." The defensive system of Bonaguil is a perfect example of a stronghold designed to resist attacks. It uses the natural formation of the limestone, with tunnels and storage areas cut out of the soft stone. As you drive through rich forests suddenly you turn a corner and there is the great fortified castle in front of you, a sight you won't forget.

Montpezat d'Agenais

The small bastide of Montpezat is where the idea of this book was conceived. My house sits across a tiny lane from the War Memorial park. Every morning and evening when I open or close my kitchen shutters I see the young man stoically staring into the distance as his hands rest on the rifle barrel. A large plane tree shades him in summer and its angular bare branches offer a bleak backdrop in winter.

Thirty-three names are carved at the base. The Gouget family lost four men—Albert, Alphonse, Arthur, and Hunyad—yet descendants of the Gouget family continue to farm the rich land surrounding the village. It is impossible for me to imagine how they survived one messenger after another notifying them of death by war.

Montpezat was an important English hub during the medieval ages. Many battles occurred in the area and eventually the powerful English duke situated at Montpezat attacked the village of Saint-Sardos. The duke discovered that the clergy there was hiding war weapons; it was unlawful to store war weapons in a village that was only a day's march to the nearest town. The duke called Montzepat's villagers to his castle where they were told of the forthcoming raid. They were given a morning porridge and bread, went to the blacksmith to sharpen their weapons, and then marched across the fields to Saint-Sardos, where they killed all the citizens. The king of France could not ignore this assault, and so began a retaliation that continued for 100 years. A cloud of war hangs over the people of Aquitaine, and farmers around Montpezat continue to find stone cannonballs in their fields.

When the French finally succeeded in capturing Aquitaine, the Montpezat castle was destroyed and its stones were used elsewhere. The villagers of Montpezat say every house, wall, and lane has some castle stones in it. Where the castle once stood, at the top of the hill, you can see remnants of the castle fortifications, a refurbished mill, as well as a model of the castle. The view is spectacular; it is a perfect spot to have a picnic or visit at sunset.

WWI 33 killed
WWII 5 killed

69

Lorette and Lisette

Penne d'Agenais

Would Richard the Lionheart, who became King of England as Richard I (1189–99), be pleased that the magnificent town he founded on top of the most commanding site along the whole of the Lot River is today visited not for its military ramparts (now in an advanced state of decay), nor for the magnificent cathedral built on their ruins, but rather for the artists and artisans who have colonized this beautiful village's houses to create their art in Richard's stronghold?

During the years I've been researching rural war memorials in southwest French towns, I've noted small but consistent changes in population. Like many small towns the youth are moving into urban areas for employment and education, cafes and shops have closed, yet for the most part the appearance of the villages remain much the same. Penne has lost some of the resident artists, but tourists consistently support the excellent restaurants and art exhibitions. During the autumn of 2017 I spent time in the car park observing whether people acknowledged the war memorial. Most did not. If they did notice the memorial, they paused long enough to read the names, maybe take a photo, and then left to explore the narrow lanes leading up the hill.

Penne lost 69 soldiers during the First World War, and the town's war memorial is not the typical stoic soldier from the same cast seen in so many French villages, nor is it an obelisk. Instead we see a profoundly sorrowful statue of Marianne, the mother of France, looking downward, holding a wreath in one hand and a palm fond in the other. Despite the hubbub of the car park all around, she stands serene in the envelope of personal quiet, remembering her sons, husbands, brothers, fathers, uncles and friends, and as we watch her we share her inner quietude.

WWI 69 killed
WWII 13 killed

1914-1918

A. ABOULY
D. ALARY
A. AVAS
A. BERTHOUMIEUX
J. BONNEFOUX
L. BOUZET
F. BROUAT
J. BRUNEL
J. BRUNET
H. BURE
E. CABEAU
L. CAPESPINE
F. CAUMONT
A. CAVAILLE
P. CENDRES
P. CHAMBANEAU
R. DE CHAZELLES DE
        BEAUREGARD
A. COLIN
J. CONSTANT
E. COSSE
L. COUDON
J. DALBY
J. DAVID

Prayssas

Prayssas is an oval thirteenth-century bastide with four gates and a twelfth-century church and tower. Go inside the church and test the acoustics, and you will understand why these old churches are perfect venues for concerts. The very pretty and well-tended village has a post office, bakery, butcher, cafes, and other shops. The houses cluster around the church and tree-lined square. You feel protected and comfortable sipping a cup of coffee or a glass of beer in the courtyard. A fountain continuously babbles softly. During August the town prepares their courtyard for the weekly night markets with local food, wine and after dark a band offers music for dancing. In the fields surrounding the village an assortment of fruit is grown. Farmers supply high-quality grapes to many local wineries but also the tiny sweet Chasselas grape, which is a delicate and delicious dessert fruit.

The war memorial is not in the town square but at the end of a long park shaded by plane trees and used for playing boules. A pale blue fence surrounds the memorial and blue artillery shell casings sit at the corners. Flags decorate the front of the pillar and a large urn is at the top. A refurbishment would benefit this memorial because some carvings on the side are too damaged for recognition.

This memorial site is especially haunting in the winter when the plane trees are pruned in the French manner. They remind me of the stark, burned, and distressed trees shown in photos of the WWI battlefields. In summer the mood is entirely different. Shade from the old grand trees offer relief from the hot sun. It is a quiet and stately place for rest, relaxation, and remembering those fallen in war. The names where the soldiers fell are carved on the side of the pillar: Dardenelles, Champagne, Somme, Marne, Verdun, Yser.

> WWI 39 killed
> WWII not recorded

Pujols

Pujols sits on a high hill overlooking the beautiful Lot valley and Villeneuve-sur-Lot. For years tourist books have named Pujols one of France's most beautiful villages. I agree. This picturesque village has preserved its medieval heritage of half-timbered houses, ancient ramparts, and vestiges of the citadel. The stronghold was destroyed after the crusade against the Albigensians and rebuilt a few decades later. The stones from Pujols were used to establish Villeneuve-sur-Lot. Today you can wander through the narrow streets, peek into the old well, admire the fortified gates, photograph the flower-covered buildings, and enjoy art shows at Sainte Foy church. On Sunday mornings, a large eclectic open market fills the village with tourists and locals shopping for local produce and handicrafts. Stop at one of the outdoor or more formal restaurants for coffee or a traditional meal.

For twenty-three years I searched in vain for the Pujols WWI war memorial. In the fall of 2017, my friend and editor Devon Musgrave visited me in France. After visiting Pujols, he took me on a different route out of Pujols and suddenly, sitting beside the road, was the beautiful memorial. Like many French war memorials, it focuses on the sorrow felt by the loved ones left behind. A young mourning woman with a headscarf covering her hair sits and gazes into eternity, pondering the misery of war.

77

Sainte-Livrade-sur-Lot

This prosperous town has my favorite Friday morning market, a very large market where you can spend several hours selecting the very freshest fruits and vegetables. A French woman told me to look at the vendors' fingernails. If they aren't dirty, the produce probably wasn't picked this morning. My favorite vendor sells roasted chicken with sautéed potatoes with or without onions. If you want something lighter, visit the ladies behind the Vietnamese stall for appetizers. After you've filled your cart with amazing food, go wander the busy lanes, similar to those in a Kasbah. You bump into friends, stumble into little kids chasing their dog, ponder over the nicely laid-out tables and tables of cloths, hats, clothes, bedding, cheap watches, toys, purses, wallets, shoes, flashlights, jewelry, and even bottle openers. You'll find something to buy from the many friendly vendors who never hassle you to make a purchase.

Sainte-Livrade is a middle-sized bastide built in the twelfth century along the Lot River. It is busy and has all the conveniences for modern life. There is an attractive stone Romanesque church where you can escape if the hustle and bustle of the market is too much for your nerves or feet. Another interesting feature is the Tour du Roy, a tower that formed part of a castle built by Richard the Lionheart. I haven't visited it yet because I'm eager to get home with my fresh food, but one day I'll find it. There are convenient coffeehouses or cafes if you need something to refresh your energy. As you stroll back to your car, take time to admire the elegant buildings that house businesses, banks, and public offices, many with intricate wrought-iron balconies.

The central square is in front of the large and impressive Hotel de Ville. It has been upgraded over the last ten years; it is a nice shady resting place where you can admire the war memorial. A decorative low fence surrounds the rather arrogant soldier who gazes into the distance. His arms are crossed across his chest and a rifle barrel is in one hand. The names of the fallen are not included, which probably means the original plaque was too damaged to include in the upgrade. The names and numbers of young men who gave their lives in WWI are known only to their loved ones.

Nicknames for the Troops

TOMMIES: This term for English soldiers came from fictional 18th century British Everyman "Tommy Atkins."

POILUS: A term meaning "hairy ones," referring to the long hair, beards, and mustaches of French soldiers of that era. Most French WWI war memorials show soldiers with mustaches.

DIGGERS: First used for Australian gold miners, then for their soldiers who dug trenches and died in the miles and miles of trenches.

DOUGHBOYS: Term for U.S. soldiers might refer to the uniform buttons that resembled unbaked bread, or it might mean that the U.S. soldiers had the"dough" to buy and eat bread.

Changes in Social Order

World War I shook up the social order of France, where a majority of the fighting occurred. Thirty six million French civilians experienced evacuations, separations, strikes, rationing of food, loss of animals, loss of housing and barns, censorship, starvation, and psychological stress. Three million females of all ages became agriculture workers on millions of French farms. They also ran the stores and became teachers, munition plant workers, war nurses, truck and tram drivers, signal corps, and other volunteers to support the war.

Internationally WWI led to the Russian Revolution and the end of the Hapsburg Monarchy and German Empire, and it restructured the political order in Europe and the Middle East. European civilians were especially bitter and weary.

Saint-Sardos

This is a small and pretty hamlet surrounding a lovely Romanesque church with a carved doorway and fading frescoes. It became an historic town when it was attacked by one of its neighboring towns, Montpezat. Saint-Sardos was a French compound and Montpezat was a very powerful English village/bastide. Officially Saint-Sardos was a religious sanctuary, and thus it was not allowed to support French soldiers or store weapons. Somehow the Duke of Montpezat heard about a cache of weapons there, and he decided to take things into his own hands. This was the prelude to the Hundred Years' War. See the "Montpezat d'Agenais" entry for more about this story.

My house is in Montpezat and I've participated in a grand festival commemorating the anniversary of the attack on Saint-Sardos. At dawn we met at the castle site for gruel and bread, walked to the blacksmith and then across the hills and fields to Saint-Sardos. A fest was in full swing with games and crafts from the Middle Ages. In the plum orchard stood rows of long tables and benches set for a traditional southwest French lunch. The weather was perfect, the food delicious, and the conversation lively. After lunch we retired to our houses for a rest and to change our clothes. In the evening we gathered again for an evening under the stars, listening to medieval music and sharing a banquet of food. It was a remarkable celebration.

For years I hunted for the war memorial here. Finally, I asked my friend Lisette to help me find the memorial. She couldn't find it either, so she asked an elderly woman hanging out her white sheets. She laughed and pointed to a small rectangle with flowers standing a few feet away. There stood the little war memorial in the middle of the roundabout. Then we had a good laugh together.

WWI 8 killed

Saint-Sylvestre-sur-Lot

On the north bank of the Lot River, Saint-Sylvestre-sur-Lot anchors the bridge that leads to Port de Penne and eventually to Penne d'Agenais on the south bank. It is an ordinary country village. There are no grand houses or beautiful parks nor hilltop views of magnificent countryside. It's just a small working town along the road.

Yet Saint-Sylvestre deserves its place here, if only because its simple pedestal memorial with the decorations of wreath, palm frond, Maltese cross, and crossed swords seen on hundreds of other memorials across France reminds us of the loss of human lives during WWI. Fifty-four young men eager to start their independent lives were snuffed out. Is that why the village is so quiet and many houses have closed shutters? What would this village be like now if it hadn't lost these young men? We will never know.

WWI 54

Savignac-sur-Leyze

If you're on the way to Monflanquin from Villeneuve-sur-Lot, it isn't far to reach Savi-gnac-sur-Leyze. When you arrive, you might think that the founders, despite the rolling acres of farmland all around, set out to create the smallest town possible as close to the road as possible which could accommodate its inhabitants. Were they hiding from Richard the Lionheart or other roaming armies? Every building is attached to every other. They crowd hard against each side of the narrow road. Ninety percent of the houses have shut their shutters in midday, which I've been told is a precaution and a tradition the farmers in southwest France established after years and years of unexpected raiding. Even the church walls are attached to the houses on each side, and its entry is a narrow passageway between two houses. Everything is neat, tidy, and well cared for, and the small church cemetery is beautifully maintained.

Consistent with the village, the war memorial is set into the wall of the church facing the road. It is completely anonymous—none of the names of the men of Savignac-sur-Leyze who fell are named. But we know some sons of the village did fall for France in the war and their loved ones wanted to remember them. If my dear Lisette were alive, she would knock on one of the doors and begin to ask questions.

Sembas

It would be an exaggeration to call Sembas a village. It is merely an old church on top of the highest hill in the immediate vicinity surrounded in spring by bright yellow fields of ripening rape. The church is small, as befits its modest location, with only two windows down each side, oriented east-west with the door to the west and, like many others in the area, its war memorial to the east behind the curved wall that surrounds the altar. All of the villages I'm describing are quiet, but Sembas, with only a simple house and a few barnlike buildings and no through traffic, is totally serene.

The memorial itself is a simple, dignified pillar. At the top is a crown with the shield of the Republic of France at its center, only barely visible now after years of erosion. Crossed swords complement the cross, and an olive branch graces the pillar below. A porcelain flower arrangement sits at the base.

Somehow sixteen people from the surrounding farms, including four with the same surname, gave their lives in the First World War for Sembas.

WWI 16
WWII 1
1955 1

How could I begin my life all over again when I had no conviction about anything except that the war was a dirty trick which had been played on me and my generation?

—Siegfried Sassoon

Tombeboeuf

You may never pass through Tombeboeuf unless you play golf. My former husband and helpmate in researching these war memorials loved golf and we occasionally visited Tombeboeuf. Later our son Jake wanted to practice golf at this very nice golf course. The town is larger than many other villages in southwest France, but at first sight it isn't a very pretty one. Sadly, it resembles many of the villages in the southwest that are struggling in the French economy due to a general movement by the youth to the larger cities. All the same, I like Tombeboeuf, with its strange name that conjures big beef steaks, even though it is a hillside town that is rather gray and tired. But make some effort to explore it. When you drive to its higher roads, you have a good view of distant rolling hills and green valleys that produce large quantities of the fruit and vegetable baskets of France.

The war memorial is quite grand. It sits upon five tiers of stone, surrounded by a hedge, and it has space to plant seasonal flowers at the base. To the side is a simple park with plane trees, but it feels a bit haphazard, as if there wasn't enough available space. The statue shows a soldier falling backward, hit in the act of tossing a grenade. He bravely holds the French flag in his left arm. It is similar to the memorial at Le Temple-sur-Lot, but the location of this memorial makes it feel more realistic.

Twenty-nine men from Tombeboeuf died in the fields of northern France. These young farmers had probably never dreamed that they would travel so far from home. The war took them and it kept them in northern France.

WWI 29 killed

WWII 1 killed

Algeria 1 killed

Tournon-d'Agenais

A stunningly beautiful town on one of the routes of the Chemin de Saint-Jacques-de-Compostelle, Tournon-d'Agenais sits on top of a high hill where you can imagine medieval peasants walking the crossroads of the Haut Pays des Seres, which now belong to Lot-et-Garonne, the Lot, and the Tarn-et-Garonne. The land consists of gentle rolling hills and valleys. It was founded by the indefatigable Alphonse de Poitiers in 1270. It is credited as a "Royal Bastide" of the thirteenth century and Charles d'Armangnac made it his capital in 1483–84. There are some half-timbered houses and arcades around the central Place du Marche. If you enjoy red wine, you might want to taste Thezac-Perricard's red wine, which was served to Nicholos II. He ordered 1000 bottles for a family party, and since then the wine's been known as the Vin du Tsar.

There are two memorials in Tournon to remember the 33 citizens who died in the First World War. One is inside Saint Barthelemy's church, built in 1886—a simple plaque on the wall besides the entry door. The other is in the public park that runs along the edge of the bastide on the hilltop with a commanding view of the rich farms far below. The memorial takes the form of a flag bearer who appears to be in the act of falling after being shot. The effect is to catch the agony of war in a precise moment that occurred many times in those fateful years. It could be the same statue as those at Le Temple-sur-Lot and Tombeboeuf.

But if the statue shows a moment of agony, the surroundings could not be more beautiful or uplifting. A beautiful garden of pansies and other spring flowers, the continuous ringing of church bells in the background, and all the while that spectacular view below. Our soldier might have died badly with his compatriots, but here his soul can rest in peace. Once again, I wished there was a bench to rest and contemplate the effects of war.

WWI 33

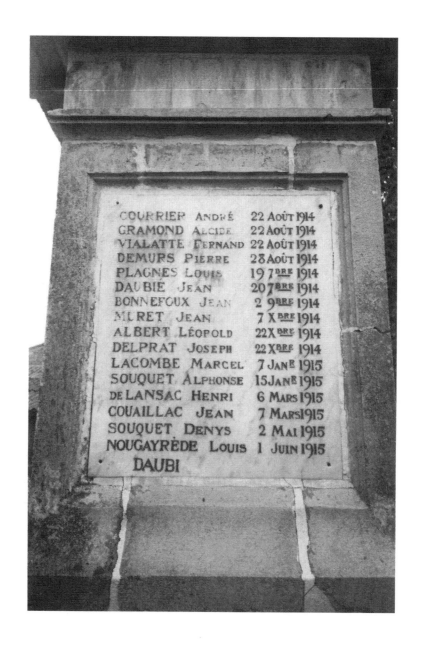

COURRIER André   22 Août 1914
GRAMOND Alcide   22 Août 1914
VIALATTE Fernand   22 Août 1914
DEMURS Pierre   28 Août 1914
PLAGNES Louis   19 7bre 1914
DAUBIE Jean   20 7bre 1914
BONNEFOUX Jean   2 9bre 1914
MURET Jean   7 Xbre 1914
ALBERT Léopold   22 Xbre 1914
DELPRAT Joseph   22 Xbre 1914
LACOMBE Marcel   7 Janr 1915
SOUQUET Alphonse   15 Janr 1915
de LANSAC Henri   6 Mars 1915
COUAILLAC Jean   7 Mars 1915
SOUQUET Denys   2 Mai 1915
NOUGAYRÈDE Louis   1 Juin 1915
DAUBI

Bent double, like old beggars under sacks,
Knock-kneed, coughing like hags, we cursed through sludge,
Till on the haunting flares we turned our backs
And towards our distant rest began to trudge.
Men marched asleep. Many had lost their boots
But limped on, blood-shod. All went lame; all blind;
Drunk with fatigue; deaf even to the hoots
Of disappointed shells that dropped behind.

Gas! GAS! Quick, boys!—An ecstasy of fumbling,
Fitting the clumsy helmets just in time;
But someone still was yelling out and stumbling
And floundering like a man in fire or lime.—
Dim, through the misty panes and thick green light
As under a green sea, I saw him drowning.

In all my dreams, before my helpless sight,
He plunges at me, guttering, choking, drowning.
If in some smothering dreams you too could pace
Behind the wagon that we flung him in,
And watch the white eyes writhing in his face,
His hanging face, like a devil's sick of sin;
If you could hear, at every jolt, the blood
Come gargling from the froth-corrupted lungs,
Obscene as cancer, bitter as the cud
Of vile, incurable sores on innocent tongues,—
My friend, you would not tell with such high zest

To children ardent for some desperate glory,
The old Lie: *Dulce et decorum est*
Pro patria mori.

—Wilfred Owen, "Dulce Et Decorum Est"

Tourtrès

Tourtrès is a very small hamlet surrounded by beautiful farm country. I often drove through this collection of houses and barns in my search of new war memorials. Tourtrès should have a memorial, but I couldn't find it in the usual places. One fine day I decided to explore the cemetery behind the very pretty church. As I opened the old gates and walked up a dirt trail, I was delighted to see this very unusual memorial honoring war casualties. A chain protects the cement base and memorial. Summer flowers grow around the base, and bronze pineapples decorate the chain posts.

On closer inspection I became mystified by the details on the tall wrought iron cross. A sign saying "mission 1862" makes me believe the families of the fallen soldiers used an existing religious sign. Underneath the mission sign is a skull with two iron pieces shaped like a V. Could that symbolize crossed bones? Above the skull is a sword and a whip. The top of the cross is decorated with at least 10 unusual symbols. There is a sun, a hand, a jug, a spear, a chalice, a moon, a bell, another differently shaped spear, and finally what appears to be pliers. Several other ornamental designs beautify the top of the cross. I suppose the marble plaque would have been added after WWI. Eight young men from this tiny hamlet did not return from war. One was killed in captivity during World War II.

Since my discovery of the Tourtrès memorial, I've seen at least two similar wrought-iron crosses with the names of the fallen on a marble plaque. Similar symbols were placed in the same positions as on the Tourtrès cross. But only the cross of Tourtrès has a skull and sign with a date.

WWI 8
WWII 1

98

Villeneuve-sur-Lot

Villeneuve-sur-Lot holds great meaning for me because my dear friend Lisette and her sister Lorette lived here and were my companions on frequent trips to find memorials. The town's symbol is its ancient bridge, Pont Vieux, which was built across the Lot in 1287 and restored in the seventeenth century. It has five spans and was once set with three fortified towers.

A special treasure is the Chapelle du Bout-du-Pont. This very, very small chapel hanging over the river made me feel dubious about entering it, but once inside I felt peaceful. The bright white walls sparkled with the sun's reflection from the river below. It was a perfect time to recall the story Lisette told me. Apparently one stormy night a boatman was caught in very rough waters and his cargo fell into the river. This was a disaster for the boatman, and he decided to dive into the water to try to save some of his goods. He made several dives into the dark and cold water but didn't find his wares. On the last dive he found a statue of the Virgin Mary. He must have been shocked but also very grateful that he survived the ordeal. Other boatmen and their families organized with the church to build this tiny chapel in gratitude to the Virgin Mary. Lorette said she remembers seeing boatmen pausing in their boats below the chapel to say a prayer before continuing their journey. Now the transport boats have disappeared and kayaks and other pleasure craft pass by the chapel.

The World War I memorial in Villeneuve-sur-Lot sits at the end of a park facing three busy streets. It is a bronze statue of a nude soldier carrying a sword while holding a fallen comrade. Behind the statue is a crescent wall with the names of the fallen. On a large black marble plaque these words are written: "La Commune de Villeneuve Sur Lot A Ses Enfants Victimes De Toutes Les Guerres." Which means "The commune of Villeneuve on the Lot to the young sons of every war."

My overall feeling while observing the refurbished memorial was a mixture of sadness, repugnance of war, and compassion for the families. How sad they were not able to see their sons develop their talents and live a normal life. The sons and families made the ultimate sacrifice.

WWI 240 killed
WWII 20 killed
WWII 6 killed in deportation
WWII 6 killed by firing squad

New War Strategies #2

BARBED WIRE: American Joseph Gladden invented barbed metal wire in 1874 for confining cattle. In WWI, barbed wire became a war implement. It protected the top of the trenches to keep enemies from entering and was spread across no-man's land, where soldiers could be easily caught and be shot by machine guns. Many WWI authors ranked barbed wire as the cheapest and most effective defensive system for a trench war.

TANKS: German soldiers saw the first fleet of British tanks in the fall of 1916. A Canadian soldier wrote, "Away to my left, a huge gray object reared itself into view, slowly, very slowly, it crawled along like a gigantic toad crossing the shell-stricken field. Down and up the shell holes it clambered, a weird, ungainly monster, moving relentlessly forward."

He didn't care because in his view nothing mattered anymore; because manners, ideas, principles even, all the ways of doing things since the war, had nothing in common with what he had known and revered for more than 60 years. In this new world children have no respect for tradition, or authority, or filial duty; in this world money, good money in gold coins, had been replaced by worthless paper. This mad world threatened by social revolutions in political struggles, this world turned upside down, no longer interested in him. He felt like a stranger who had lost his way.

—Reactions of a 60-year-old Frenchman after World War I, as written by Claude Michelet, *Firelight and Woodsmoke* (1993)

Villereal

Years ago my Montpezat neighbors, Dr. Alain Lafage and his wife, Jakie, introduced me to the charms of Villereal. I was smitten at first sight. Villereal is one of nearly 300 fortified bastides built in southwestern France between 1220 and 1370 by the counts of Toulouse and King Edward 1 of England. Bastides were designed to protect the citizens from enemies as well as provide economic and political opportunities. Peasants were awarded land in exchange for their support of the bastide founder. Villereal's thirteenth-century fortified church has two turrets connected by a wall walk. A drawbridge was used to enter the village until the seventeenth century. The town square is expansive enough for a two-storied covered market building made of hand-honed beams and half-timbered cob walls.

The second story of the market was where money could be exchanged and in some cases wares were stored. This was a great advancement over the wet, muddy, uncovered town squares in older villages. Other improvements were the wide main streets to facilitate carts and small streets between houses to prevent fires from spreading. Surrounding the market square were two-storied houses, the upper floor the living quarters and the ground floor a workshop or a shopkeeper's store.

On many visits to Villereal I failed to find the WWI memorial. Finally, on my 2017 visit a gracious lady in the coffee shop gave me directions. Villereal's memorial is unique, standing majestically in an impressive park along the main road. On top of a very tall obelisk a sorrowful Mother of France looks down, her wings are spread wide and one hand holds a wreath. A metal peace branch with a depiction of a French soldier decorates the obelisk. There are six steps up to the white marble plaque with these words:

A LA MEMOIRE GLORIEUSE
DES SOLDATS DE
VILLEREAL

Lower down a second marble plaque lists the names of 75 fallen soldiers from four communes. Six families lost two members. A smaller white marble plaque recognizes the seven fallen soldiers of WWII.

PART 2:
SOUTHEAST AUSTRALIA

LIST OF TOWNS

Adelaide

This very pretty city is the capital of the state of South Australia and the fifth most populous city in Australia. The total population of South Australia is only 1.7 million, and more than 75% of the people live in the greater Adelaide area. The National War Memorial honoring the 28,000 men who served in the First World War is in the city center on the Government House grounds. It is called the National War Memorial even though only South Australian soldiers are named. Scholar Ken Inglis suggests that the name may have reflected the idea, which is still held by many, that the "province is a nation."

The memorial was funded by the Parliament of South Australia. A rigorous competition in 1924 produced 26 designs, but all were lost when a fire destroyed the building where they were stored. A majority of the judging was completed before the fire, and the committee claimed that none of the proposals were suitable. A second competition in 1926 set out greater clarity as to the requirements, and 18 new entries were submitted.

The selected design shows two scenes depicting the "prelude and epilogue to war." One side focuses on the willingness of youth to answer the call of duty, and the other side demonstrates the large sacrifices they made. This memorial does not present a material victory but a victory of the spirit.

For seven years, little progress was made toward the final decision for the memorial. Political battles ensued due to political pressures and controversies over the new ideas. Pressure from the returned soldiers got the ball rolling again. Construction began in 1928, and when it opened in 1931, the memorial was Australia's fourth state WWI memorial. It was unveiled before a crowd of almost 75,000 on Anzac Day. The crowd was unable to fit in front of the memorial, so many thousands gathered at the Cross of Sacrifice in Pennington Gardens, dedicated in 1923 by donations raised by the League of Loyal Women.

The finished structure has two sides, referred to by the architects as "reverse and obverse, or prologue and epilogue of war." Each side features a relief carved from Angaston marble and framed by the "rough-hewn" arch carved out of marble. Granite steps lead up to the monument.

The north side of the monument, or prologue, features a relief of the Spirit of Duty as a vision before the youth of South Australia. It shows three figures—a girl, a student, and a farmer—each abandoning the "symbols of their craft." They are in normal dress, not yet soldiers. They face away from the world as they look to the vision. The Spirit of Duty shows a female figure in an Art Deco style, which was new in Australia at the time. On the reverse side of the monument is a relief carving showing the Spirit of Compassion holding a stricken soldier. Beneath the figure is a Fountain of Compassion. The flow of water represents the "constant flow of memories," and the fountain's lion's head, bearing the Imperial Crown, represents the British Commonwealth of Nations.

Within the memorial are bronze plaques listing the names of the soldiers who served in the Great War. The design honors both the war dead and those who served in the war. Over the doors are names of the locations of the major battles in which Australian soldiers fought.

Adjacent to the National War Memorial are additional but smaller monuments. One is the Memorial to the Battle of Lone Pine, where a tree from the original lone pine grows beside a small plaque. The French Memorial, unveiled in 1993, honors the South Australians who died in France during the first and second World Wars. Not on the grounds with the National War Memorial but equally important is a memorial arch leading to the pier. "ARCH OF REMEMBRANCE" is written over the gateway to the water, a place where people walk daily to and from Adelaide's beaches.

Angaston

Angaston is one of my favorite towns in South Australia. It is about 77 km. NE of Adelaide and was founded in 1842. My family and I celebrated my 60th birthday at the charming and comfortable Angus homestead. We enjoyed breakfast on the veranda watching the birds and butterflies, and dinner was served in the elegant yet homey dining room. The Angus family left the original furniture and books. Before dinner my former husband Greg read Greek stories while we enjoyed the evening mood on the veranda. We sipped delicious local wine and a fine selection of hors-d'oeuvres. During the day we visited the town of Angaston, and I discovered the grand bronze WWI memorial.

The town of Angaston was named after C.H. Angas, a prosperous land owner. The streets are lined with traditional Australian buildings, many with verandas to provide shade and coolness for those walking by. The restaurants are excellent and the wine is superb. The Barossa valley produces some of the best deep red wines in Australia. German migrants to Australia started growing grapes, among other crops, in the late 1880s. It's a joke among Australians that if the wine is good it will remain in Australia. (There is a parallel between the Barossa valley and southwest France since both produce excellent wines and fruit.) I must point out that during WWI the German immigrants were not allowed to speak the German language, many Lutheran schools were closed for fear they might be teaching propaganda, frequently Germans were interned, and all immigration of German people was stopped between 1914–25. Discrimination comes in many colors.

The war memorial sits in a small green manicured plot once owned by the late Mr. George Fife Angas. The park is at a junction of two roads, so the war memorial is very visible. The monument is a bronze statue of the Archangel Michael, approximately 18 feet tall, holding a wreath above his head and in his left hand a crusader's sword. This dramatic figure sits on a pink Angaston marble pedestal. Bronze plaques lists more than one hundred names, all enlisted men from the district. The monument is surrounded by a circular rose garden.

Apollo Bay

Apollo Bay is a small town around a beautiful crescent bay on the Great Ocean Road. It's a small town, but there is a monument to the men who served in the Great War. (The term "Great War" is frequently used in Australia.) In the late 1990s I was joined by two good friends from the French village where my house is located. We drove from Melbourne along the Great Ocean Road into South Australia, stopping at the Great Otway National Park and walking through a bushy forest toward the lighthouse on Cape Otway. We didn't reach the light house because it was growing dark, but we admired the magnificent blue ocean and sandy broad beach while tramping through the wild bush land of the Otway Ranges.

Apollo Bay was part of the land of the aboriginal people called Gudubanud, who are now gone. In the 1840s a whaling station was established and soon more settlers arrived and cut timber and worked in sawmills. In the early years the only access to the bay was by sea.

The war memorial is a simple but clearly cut statue of an Australian solider in uniform, his hands resting on a rifle. He stares straight ahead in the same stoic manner as many men on French war memorials. The difference is the cocky Australian hat perched at an angle—it seems to represent the Australian soldier's spirit. These young men were described as hard working, tough as nails, good companions, and resourceful in finding creative solutions under difficult situations. Most had grown up on farms or sheep and cattle ranges in the outback where doing heavy and complicated tasks in tough climate conditions and rugged terrain was the norm.

This memorial stands along the road with evergreen trees behind it. There aren't any roses, green grass, or benches. The serious young man stands alone, quietly remembering and representing his fallen buddies. Sadly, I don't have the number of soldiers listed on the pedestal. The biblical quote from John 15, verse 13 is carved into the stone, "Greater love hath no man than this, that he lay down his life for his friends." It was erected by the residents of Apollo Bay and District and made by Nash from Geelong, Victoria. On the back is a section with the names of those lost in World War II.

Avoca

Avoca is located about 100 miles NE of Melbourne near the gold-mining district surrounding Ballarat. It is one of two main towns in the Pyrenees Shire, the other being Beaufort to the south. The history of Avoca has a dark center. The early settlers did not assimilate with the Dja Dja Wurnung people, whose land they were using. In Blood Hole at Middle Creek there was a massacre in 1839–40. A great number of Dja Dja aboriginals were killed. Similar stories are not uncommon in Australian history.

By 1850 there were several large sheep runs and acres of pasture. Then came the discovery of gold in the Pyrenees Ranges near Avoca. Over the next several years the population grew from 100 to 2,200 and Avoca became an administrative center. In the late 20th century the region became known as the gateway to the Pyrenees wine region.

The Avoca Soldiers' Memorial is prominent in the city park. Built in 1921, it was originally a band stand with eight pillars supporting the roof. A frieze above the columns shows the names where the soldiers fought: Gallipoli, France, Palestine, Belgium. On the low walls a soldier's helmet and pack are sculpted in realistic high relief. The other sides have granite tablets with the names of those who fought. A tablet on the north side lists the names of the men who died.

It was a beautiful day when I visited Avoca, the skies a brilliant blue. It was lunch time so I ate my sandwich on a nearby bench while admiring this unique war memorial. It was clean and well-tended with low shrubs and green grass. My spirits were uplifted as I paused to observe the park, nearby buildings, and this beautiful and touching memorial. What an impressive way for the Avoca citizens to pay homage to the men who served and died in the Great War.

WWI The Fallen (killed) 33		
2 named Brown		
WWI Roll of Honor (enlisted and returned) 107		
2 named Brereton	2 named Gee	3 named Kitchell
2 named Burke	2 named Golber	2 named Leydon
2 named Chandler	2 named Greenwood	2 named McVicar
2 named Cross	2 named Harbowfield	2 named Randall
2 named Doodt	3 named Henderson	2 named Wilson
2 named Elliott	3 named Jardine	2 named Willmott
3 named French	5 named Johnson	2 named Withered

The Battle of Gallipoli

The ANZAC forces (Australian, New Zealand, and Canada) under British leadership fought courageously and suffered dire losses in a long battle of attrition. The Gallipoli Campaign resembled the Western Front, with trenches and neither side able to break the deadlock.

Many Australians and Kiwis point to their countrymen's sacrifices at Gallipoli as building their national awareness and pride while becoming a part of the world stage. By the end of 1915 the troops were withdrawn. The evacuation of 135,000 soldiers began in December and ended on January 9, 1916. Most ANZAC troops returned to battles in France.

Australian Epitaphs

More than 60,000 Australian soldiers, servicewomen, and nurses did not return and are buried in graves in France, Belgium, Britain, Gallipoli, Palestine (now modern Israel, Jordan, and parts of Syria), and Egypt. Per capita, Australian lost more soldiers than any other country in WWI. Being unable to visit the grave sites, Australian families were allowed to write a 66-letter epitaph for the grave stone. New Zealand decided to not have epitaphs, nor do the French and Belgium grave markers carry epitaphs.

Australian epitaphs offer a variety of emotions, attitudes, and tastes that reflect an Australian atmosphere. Imagine how difficult it would be to select words for your loved one buried in a country you will probably never visit. The father, mother, wife sitting at a table, their heart breaking but trying to express their love in 66 letters. I marvel at these words of love.

TOO FAR AWAY, THY GRAVE TO SEE, BUT NOT TOO FAR, TO THINK OF THEE

BEHOLD FRANCE, THOU HOLDEST ONE OF AUSTRALIA'S BRAVEST AND BEST

HE GAVE HIS LIFE, FOR FRANCE AND LIBERTY

NOTHING ON EARTH, CAN EVER REPAY, FOR THE SACRIFICE,
HE MADE THAT DAY

THEY LAID HIM BY, WITH PRAYER AND SIGH, THE SPOT WHERE HE WAS KILLED

NO PEN CAN WRITE, NO TONGUE CAN TELL, THE LOSS OF HIM,
I LOVED SO WELL

THOUGH IN A FOREIGN LAND, YOU LIE, OUR LOVE FOR YOU WILL NEVER DIE

Bealiba and Districts

Bealiba is a town in the state of Victoria, located in the Central Goldfields Shire about 129 miles NW of Melbourne and 46 miles from Bendigo. In the 1840s Bealiba was home to drovers. The first permanent settler was George Coutts in 1845. Everything changed when gold was discovered in 1856. After 18 months of the gold rush Bealiba grew to 18,000 persons. After the gold rush, framers were invited to set up operations.

Bealiba is a small town but has a pub, post office and general store. There are some buildings of historic interest from 1857, and the town hall was built in 1879. It was a hot day when I searched for the war memorial, and no one else appeared on the street. But I wasn't alone. All I had to do was look up at the broad bright blue sky showing off its billows of white clouds resembling nesting hens. I felt like singing "Oh What A Beautiful Morning." My heart sang with gratitude to be in this amazing landscape.

Small towns in Australia are usually quiet, much like the charming small villages in southwest France, yet they share a common history. Many of their sons lie together in French war graves.

Bealiba's war memorial was simple, clear, and thought-provoking. A simple stone pillar with a rough rounded top. It simply lists the names of the fallen soldiers. At the top of the monument are these words:

FOR KING AND COUNTRY BEALIBA AND DISTRICTS TRIBUTE TO ITS
FALLEN SOLDIERS WHO DIED FOR THE EMPIRE IN THE WAR 1914–1919

WWI 96 fallen		
WWII none were listed		
The following indicate the names with more than one person listed on the memorial		
3 Bumstead	3 Lyndon	2 Scullery
2 Collison	2 Harrop	4 Sheen
2 Collins	2 Quintile	2 Simons
2 Drayton	2 Parker	2 Stevenson
3 Holt	2 Ross	3 Wishart

Berwick

Berwick was named after a town in Scotland and is now a suburb of Melbourne 25 miles from the city center. Originally it was part of the Cardina Creek run, and in 1854 the first settlers began to set up farms and businesses in the beautiful rolling hills surrounding Berwick, including many dairies. In the 20th century Melbourne began to spread toward Berwick, yet some of the traditional buildings of the Victorian era remain. One is the Border Inn that was licensed in 1857 and remains as the Berwick Inn. It was an important social center for the citizens in the early days and a rest stop for coaches traveling to Gippsland. Although I wasn't able to visit the botanical garden, I've been told it is a treasure of beauty and tranquility.

Poplar trees line High Street and were planted as an Avenue of Honor for the fallen in the First World War. Originally name plaques were to be mounted at the foot of each tree but that was never accomplished. The War Memorial takes center stage. It sits proudly in the boulevard park with trees growing on both streets. A five-tiered granite pedestal stands on a raised stone square. Potted plants anchor each corner and a lion carved out of white stone gazes outward as if on guard. On both front and back sides of the memorial landing are three steps with a graceful handrail to guide you up to the monument's base. I must have visited here in the spring because my photos show green grass covering the landing and roses blooming in the village gardens.

On the front of the pedestal twenty names are carved into the stone with the dates 1914–1919. Below is a second carving of 1939–1945 with seven names written. On the back of the monument is a new plaque with a medallion showing soldiers and possibly female nurses.

Borung Shire

In 1911 the small town of Borung's population was listed as 177 persons. Borung is also the name of the nearest highway. Very few highway names in the state of Victoria have Aboriginal names, but in the 19th century Mr. W.E. Stanbridge befriended the Booroung people while studying Aboriginal astronomy. It is thought that is how the highway was named. "Borung" means "the broad-leafed mallee scrub." Borung is now in the Warracknabeal Shire. I use "Borung Shire" because that is the name on the WWI memorial.

The memorial sits in the fenced city park surrounded by large gum and palm trees. The gate to the park is the war memorial. Two large square pillars with globes on the top anchor the big black wrought iron gate. Two smaller pillars stand beside the taller pillars making a smaller passage through smaller gates. The two large pillars and the smaller pillars list the names of the men who fought in the war. Eighty-four names appear on the four pillars. It is important to remember that Australia usually honors all who fought in the war, not just those who died, and Borung was a Shire, so these men came from more than the small town of Borung. But even given these facts, 84 is a staggeringly large number of men from this area sent overseas to fight.

Another stone pillar, standing by itself, lists the names of 32 men who fought in World War II, which occurred after Borung was no longer a Shire, so Warracknabeal Shire dedicated the WWII monument. A smaller stone pillar made of similar stone stands alone. It honors the men and women who fought in Korea, Borneo, Malaya, and Vietnam.

Not far from the gates and pillars a large German cannon stands, most certainly a war trophy. There was no story to describe the weapon. An empty flag pole stood to one side.

The park was peaceful and spacious with white benches for resting and enjoying the peace and quiet. Flower beds were well-tended, but not many flowers bloom in the heat of an Australian summer. Not a single person walked through the park while I made photos and notes.

WWI 84
WWII 32

Brighton

Brighton is a popular upmarket suburb of Melbourne. It has a very nice shopping area with restaurants, bars, bakeries, butchers, and vegetable/fruit stores. It sits on a long stretch of light-tan sandy beach well known for the 82 colorful bathing boxes that are almost identical to the ones erected 100 years ago. They are architecturally consistent, maintained, and painted in bright cheerful colors. You are fortunate to have one of these popular bathing boxes.

The war memorial is large and sits in a green park overlooking the beach and sea. It is made of large cream-colored stone blocks forming a fortress-like base and a tall obelisk rising high into the sky. It is a favorite resting place for the local seagulls. High on the obelisk is probably a bronze shield and lower down are these words:

ERECTED IN HONOR OF THOSE WHO FOUGHT IN THE GREAT WAR 1914–1919.

A large bronze sculpture depicts a wreath, burning lamp, a sword, two different types of rifles, and what might be palm branches. Carved into the stone is the enlarged word "SERVICE." It is somber and monumental but without individual names. There are two resting benches, one facing the water and the other the monument. It is a lovely spot.

Further away is a war trophy of a large black cannon. It quietly reminds me that war is all about killing and destruction. I lived in Brighton for seven years and walked my dogs to the beach. We often paused at the war memorial, and other times I ignored it. Do we have to avoid the hard questions of war from time to time? How do I balance my appreciation and sorrow for the loss of so many people, soldiers and civilians, with my hate of war? Growing up I remember men saying, "War is good for the economy." I never heard them say, "What a loss. Just think if we had the skills and talents of those we lost."

132

Fred

Bulla

Bulla is another small town about 18 miles north of Melbourne's city center, but its local government is in the City of Hume. Early on the name was Bulla Bulla with Deep Creek flowing through the township. It is recorded that Bulla's name has indigenous origins. "Bulla bulla," which means "two round low hills" or "the two breasts" are Aboriginal descriptions of Bulla. When you see the geography, it isn't difficult to imagine both representations.

One of the first settlers was William Wright in 1843, nicknamed "Tulip" because he had a fine collection of tulips. Gradually other settlers built a flour mill, brickwork and pottery shop, and the large Bulla Cream Company. For many years Bulla was the largest town in the region. A substantial bluestone townhall is on the main street. Nearby is the Alister Clark Memorial Rose Garden, and a short distance away you can visit his house "Glenara" and the nearly complete collection of surviving roses he loved and improved that they might thrive in Australian climates. I often bought Alister Clark's roses for our olive grove "Lovers Chase" near Lancefield, a town north of Bulla.

Near Bulla is a place called Diggers Rest. I wondered if it was named for the WWI "diggers," as Australian soldiers were frequently called. But this Diggers Rest was a stopping place for people going to the Bendigo goldfields.

The simple, dignified war memorial stands beside the Sunbury road in Bulla. It was dedicated in 1920, which is very soon after the end of the war. Most war memorials took more than a year just for sorting out the politics connected with the "where, what, who, and how" for the final memorial and site. It is a medium-sized obelisk with four layers of stone. Smaller columns stand guard at each corner. Grass surrounds it, but there aren't any flowers, trees, or resting places. Two sections of names are listed under the titles of DECEASED SOLDIERS and RETURNED SOLDIERS. It is a solemn and straightforward memorial without any wreaths, flags, or decoration. A very small red, white, and blue southern cross flag was stuck in a crack of the monument. It helped relieve the sadness I felt as I gazed at the names. Another part of me asked, "Why is it so easy for humans to forget?"

WWI 9 killed
28 returned
2 names of Daniel
2 names of Grant
2 names of Lane

Erected By the Residents
—Of Bulla—
IN HONOR OF THE MEN WHO FOUGHT
FOR THE EMPIRE IN THE
GREAT WAR 1914-1919
DECEASED SOLDIERS

GRANT M.A.   LYON W.J.
HILL S.   MANSFIELD P.
JOHNSON J.W.L.   RALSTON W.J.
LANE A.E.   RICHARDS H.C.
TATE E.J.

RETURNED SOLDIERS.
ANDREWS J.   GREIG R.
DANIEL H.H.   HARDY E.T.
DANIEL S.T.   HEWARD F.L.
DOLAN W.   LANE A.V.
FANNING J.   LANE H.A.
GILLIGAN T.L.   MALLON F.
GRANT B.H.   MILLAR H.J.
GRAY E.L.   NEAL K.

A Young German Girl's Diary

Piete Kuhr is twelve-year-old girl from east Prussia, just a few miles away from Russian troops on the Eastern Front. Below are excerpts from her daily diary.

The teachers say we must stop using foreign words.

Sentries with loaded rifles guard the railway station and sometimes fire a shot or two. The bayonets are long and thinner than I thought. They say the Russians will blow up the station.

I feel the enemy are near. People are uneasy and fresh refugees arrived from East Prussia. Some are well dressed, others not. They carry bundles and suitcases, bedding, coats all tied together. One woman looks at me and says "You don't know what this is like." Some are in horse-drawn carts but most are on foot.

More refugees come and most babies' bottoms are red because the mothers don't have dry nappies. We give them old sheets and shirts.

When we win a battle we have a day off from school.

More and more people are fleeing. The train station is swarming with wailing refugees. A woman with a black headband is crying because she lost her daughter, and an old man grabs my grandma and asked if she's seen a little girl in a blue coat. He explains he is nearly blind. We feed them bread, coffee, and soup.

Burnside District

Situated in a leafy green park in the Burnside District is a remarkable and dramatic bronze statue by Australian sculptor C. Web Wilbert. It commemorates the soldiers who died in service or were killed in WWI battles. Later a plaque was added to honor those who died in WWII, the Korean War, and the Vietnam War. The World War I soldier leans forward with his left arm extended as if helping a mate to "go over the top" or "hop the bags" as he enters no man's land for battle. His right arm is stretched behind and his hand holds onto his rifle for balance. The expression on his face is stoic and compassionate. Australian troops were admired for their support of their fellows. Pausing to help a fellow soldier while standing at the top of a trench puts him in danger, yet he stoops to help the other soldier climb up and over. That admirable quality of honor, even under extreme stress. is beautifully conceived by the sculptor. There is some oxidation of the bronze but I like the effect—you can imagine the sweat and mud smeared on the weary soldier.

Because the statue appears to be modeled on a WWI diorama showing the attack on St. Quentin, also designed by C. Webb Gilbert, this monument focuses on the French western front, not on Gallipoli. It was unveiled December 14, 1924, five years after the end of the Great War. The statue is at the end of a long park lined with trees planted in honor of the soldiers. Eighty-seven trees with a plaque at the foot of each tree stand for the men who stood at attention and then followed the orders to march bravely ahead and possibly die. Avenues of Honor such as this one are among the most poignant representations of the enormous sacrifices made by young men.

The top plaque says, "BURNSIDE DISTRICT FALLEN SOLDIERS MEMORIAL FOR THE GREAT WAR, 1914–1918." Below are three plaques listing the 87 names of the fallen soldiers on three sides of the monument. At the front of the statue is a long, paved walking path with an enclosed outline of a cross built into the tiles.

> WWI 87 killed
>
> 2 names of Sands
>
> 2 names of Shepley
>
> 2 names of Slope
>
> 2 named of Shard
>
> 2 names of Tucker
>
> 2 names of Frerechs
>
> 2 names of Hughes
>
> 2 names of Keel

Charlotte

Carisbrook

Carisbrook is a small town in the Central Goldfields Shire located in the central part of Victoria state. Its population in 2006 was 713 persons. Buses connect Carisbrook to the larger towns of Maryborough and Castlemane. The town maintains a weekly newspaper and supports a local Australian Rules Football team.

The World War I memorial is situated in a large park with typical gum and other native trees giving comforting shade. The large grey stone obelisk sits on red gravel and has a simple chain fence almost surrounding it. One side of the fence is missing. There are three steps at the base of the obelisk that some authors say represent God, King, and Country. The front side of the monument is carved with the following message:

IN MEMORY OF THE BRAVE AND
NOBLE DEAD OF CARISBROOK AND DISTRICT.
1914–1919

Twenty-three names are carved in the monument stone walls. The following message is written below the names:

PASS NOT THIS STONE IN SORROW BUT IN PRIDE—
MAY YOU LIVE AS NOBLY AS THEY DIED.

On the obelisk's backside the following is carved into the monument:

> 1939–1945
>
> J. Baker
>
> W.J. Baker
>
> G.M. Biggen
>
> Lest we Forget
>
> unveiled by Bri. Gen. Brand Feb 2–1921

It was a warm day and long shadows fell across the brown grass. I longed for a bench to sit upon and to ponder the space and monument. Walking around, I noticed, as much by sound as sight, small insect-like creatures hopping freely across the dry grass. There was a melancholy mood, similar to how I feel at the end of summer and before autumn breaks out with vibrant colors. There is an indescribable smell and feeling that tells me summer is slowly coming to the end.

Colbinabbin

The name Colbinabbin has two very different interpretations, both derived from aboriginal dialects. One is "the meeting of red and black soils," which makes sense since Mt. Camel to the south of Colbinabbin has red volcanic soil. The second interpretation is "dingo caught in a trap." Colbinabbin sits along a road leading to Bendigo, Vic. There are some small shops along the main road and nice traditional shaped Australian country houses. One older house for sale has the tin roof, a covered veranda, and the long wraparound porch where you can rest with a cup of tea and enjoy the afternoon breezes under shade. The garden is overgrown with wild flowers, weeds, and dry grass, and an old pump sits forlorn in the yard. It appears to be vacant but reflects its elegant past. It was built by David Mitchell, a Melbourne builder and father to the famous singer Dame Nellie Melba. The popular Downton Abbey TV series had a visit by Dame Melba to the Downton Abbey house. She wasn't considered acceptable to join the guests for dinner, but Clara went up and invited her all the same. Eventually she joined the dinner party and of course impressed everyone with her charm, beauty, and, most of all, intelligence.

The War Memorial is tall and trim, like a young pretty 16-year-old girl waiting for life to begin. It honors those from the district who served in WWI and those from the district who fell. It was difficult to determine the accurate number of fallen due to damage to the names. I estimate 36 soldiers were lost. A second list of names honor the men and women who enlisted from Colbinabbin and District and lost their lives in the WWII.

This elegant obelisk sits in a city park with a picnic table and a children's playground nearby. The grass was tinged a yellow green color and in the distance the big native trees towered toward the pale blue wide sky. I visited the memorial in the late afternoon and the temperature was high. Maybe that explains the absence of people in the park. At the base of the monument there were three very colorful and freshly presented bouquets, probably laid there in memory of ANZAC day.

Derrinallum

Situated in a pastoral flat farming area, Derrinallum is a peaceful small town located on the Hamilton Highway. The lush rich farmland lies at the foot of Mount Elephant, which is a 240-meter-high extinct volcano. I couldn't see much of an elephant in the volcano, but it is an impressive backdrop for the town. In the 2006 census Derrinallum had a population of 557. Over the summer the town hosts a country farmers market once a month. The main avenue is flanked with elm trees and a grass park between two streets. The town serves the surrounding farms involved in cropping, grazing, wool, sheep, cattle, and some dairying.

Derrinallum's war memorial sits in the boulevard city park flanked by the gracious elm trees. It is a peaceful space. The young soldier gazes forward with his back upright as if ready for orders. It is an excellent example of the traditional WWI Australian war uniform. While I study the young man's face and stance I can't help thinking how young he looks. Why did he want to go to war? Was it for God, King and Country? Or was it because he wanted to experience something new and see the world far from Australia?

There are three tiers of stone with a bronze wreath on the top. Beneath the soldier the word "Gallipoli" is carved into the stone, along with "To Our Glorious Dead 1914–1918." No names are listed. "EGYPT" is written on the left side, and the back inscription says:

IN MEMORY OF THOSE FROM DERRENALLUM AND
DISTRICT WHO FELL IN THE 1939–1945 WAR

FRANCE is written on the right side, plus these words:

TO HONOR OUR FALLEN WOUNDED AND THOSE WHO SUFFERED
IN WWII, KOREA, MALAYSIA, BORNEO, VIETNAM

As I walk away, I'm happy we have this monument to remember the agony of war, but I wonder if it will make a major difference in the decisions our leaders make regarding war.

Dunkeld

The Chapwurrung people lived in this region over 4000 years prior to the arrival of the Europeans. As the newcomers bought land for raising sheep, conflicts occurred between the original people and Europeans. Violent fighting killed many aboriginals. Most of the newcomers were Scottish and named the town after a Scottish town founded during Roman times. The new Dunkeld thrived in the mid-19th century from making wool. Wherever you stand in Dunkeld, at least one of the Grampian Mountains looms above you. Mt. Sturgeon has the most craggy face, domineering a landscape of flat farmland full of sheep or gangs of eastern grey kangaroos.

The memorial stands at the center of the town in the spacious and tidy Dunkeld and District Memorial Park. Manufactured by Barklamb Brothers, it was dedicated in August 1929. It is a tall monument with a sober Australian soldier made of white marble on the top of a sandstone "temple" made of pale pink stone, probably from the Grampians. He looks weary and sad but the cocky happy-go-lucky Australian hat shows a sense of pride for a job well done. Within the temple is a granite block with gilded letters:

ERECTED BY THE RESIDENTS OF DUNKELD AND DISTRICT IN HONOR OF THOSE WHO SERVED IN THE GREAT WAR 1914–1919 AS A LASTING TRIBUTE TO THE MEMORY OF THOSE WHO GAVE THEIR LIVES. WE LIE DEAD IN MANY LANDS THAT YOU LIVE HERE IN PEACE.

It was a cloudy day when I visited. The sky was the soldier's background and it was not the usual bright blue Australian sky but rather somber grey. That was appropriate for how the statue made me feel. The statue is given a sense of protection by a low fence and spacious area filled with gravel, but I couldn't shake the feeling of loneliness. There wasn't another person in the park admiring the emotional and elegant memorial.

WWI 36 killed
2 named Brady
2 named Cameron
2 named Dark
3 named Middleton
4 named Williams
3 named Womersley
WWII 10 killed
2 named McLeod

Dunolly and Bet Bet District

Dunolly originally belonged to the Dja Dja Warring people who named it Lea Kuribur. There wasn't any recorded fighting between the aboriginal and newcomers. In 1886 an unknown prospector recounted the discovery of gold. In a week the population of Dunolly jumped from 12 to 2,000. The author said it took him eight days to sink the shaft for gold and it didn't produce, so he went elsewhere. In those eight days the population had grown to 80,000. This story might be an exaggeration, of course.

The history of Dunolly is murky. The township moved four times before the gold rush. Today's town is the fifth location and was founded in 1863. It is a thriving country town, and the surrounding area remains a popular place to fossick for gold with metal detectors.

The Shire of Bet Bet was abolished in 1995, but its name remains on the World War I War Memorial in Dunolly. Most likely it was named from an Aboriginal word meaning place of red ochre. The memorial pillar is located in front of the town hall on Broadway. It is topped by an urn and rests on a square concrete plinth or step. It lists 94 locals who died in WWI. The pillars appear to be made of red marble with gold letters. There isn't much space around the memorial. In fact, it appears squashed between a grassy space with the sidewalk on one side and parked cars on the other side. The back of the monument faces a deserted fenced-in field. Yet the details on the monument are still in good condition, except for one side of the pillar. On the front are these words:

> LOOK NOT AT THIS STONE IN SORROW, BUT IN PRIDE,
> THAT YOU MAY LIVE AS NOBLE AS THEY DIED

On three sides of the pillar the names of the 94 fallen are listed.

WWI 94 killed
2 named Anderson
2 named Brett
3 named Briccs
2 named Bell
2 named Came
2 Hennessy
2 Ragnell

150

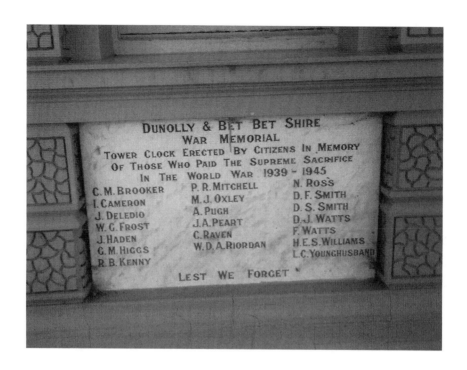

DUNOLLY & BET BET SHIRE
WAR MEMORIAL
TOWER CLOCK ERECTED BY CITIZENS IN MEMORY
OF THOSE WHO PAID THE SUPREME SACRIFICE
IN THE WORLD WAR 1939 - 1945

C. M. BROOKER   P. R. MITCHELL   N. ROSS
I. CAMERON   M. J. OXLEY   D. F. SMITH
J. DELEDIO   A. PUGH   D. S. SMITH
W. G. FROST   J. A. PEART   D. J. WATTS
J. HADEN   C. RAVEN   F. WATTS
G. M. HIGGS   W. D. A. RIORDAN   H. E. S. WILLIAMS
R. B. KENNY   L. C. YOUNGHUSBAND

LEST WE FORGET

Charlie

Killmore

Kilmore is 37 miles north of Melbourne and a short distance from our olive grove in Lancefield. Developers of another olive grove near Kilmore were always helpful in answering my many questions related to olives. Eventually we bought an olive press from them. It was fun to visit bustling Kilmore, get supplies and a cup of coffee. At the time I didn't know they claimed to be Victoria's oldest inland town. Their proof was that the Kilmore Post Office was opened on February 1, 1843, but the claim is contested by the residents of Wangaratta, another inland town that claims it was established on the same day.

The memorial for WWI and WWII is in the city park, surrounded by large trees that provide a green, cool and peaceful space. A low stone semi-circle wall is behind the memorial, offering a sense of security. The grey obelisk stands on a three-step landing and at each corner is a short pillar.

ANZAC Day in Kilmore is celebrated each year by inviting a prominent speaker to talk about the war. Last year the speaker not only talked about soldiers who died during WWI, but he compared the facts on the war memorial with new information revealed by modern technology. Often new facts dramatically change the picture of the fighting in WWI. In the 1900s young Australian boys had few career and travel opportunities. In an interview I read in a recent article about a 102-year-old veteran of WWI, it was possible he joined the forces due to peer pressure or desire to travel. In the interview he said, "I guess it was because others were doing it, and I'd be able to see the world." And these boys were still loyal citizens of the British Empire and wanted to prove their love for "King, Country, and God." But did they understand what that meant? We know they were eager to join the forces even if they were below the age limit. They exaggerated their age in hopes of passing the strict recruiting criteria.

I was impressed with the Kilmore speaker and how he provided an excellent avenue to present day students to compare their own reality with teenage boys who lived in the early 1900s. These discussions are an opportunity to open a dialogue or comparisons between life conditions and expectations for similar-aged boys who are living a hundered years apart. Isn't that what it means to remember and share with future generations?

Kyneton

In the 19th century the English explorer Thomas Mitchell came near the present town of Kyneton in 1836. The first British settlers arrived in the area the same year. A post office was established in 1843. Kyneton was not a gold rush town since it was officially established in 1850 and the gold rush began in 1851. Kyneton did become a major stop for those headed to the gold fields, and many local merchants benefitted from the gold rush. The town was first named Mt. Macedon, after the Macedon mountain ranges, but renamed Kyneton in 1854, after an English village in Warwickshire.

Kyneton is a thriving town about an hour's drive north of Melbourne. A botanical garden established in the mid 1800s offers picnic areas and many walking paths along the Campaspe River. After shopping and enjoying lunch in a trendy restaurant, visitors can admire the historic houses, many made of traditional bluestone. The beautiful Mt. Macedon Mountains are a stone's throw away. Kyneton has an annual ANZAC Day parade and a Daffodil Festival.

The Kyneton WWI War Memorial is located in the city center. The large stone obelisk sits on three large stone steps and four raw cut stone pillars stand at each corner with a chain connecting the pillars. The obelisk's front shows two swords pointing to the earth and a ribbon wrapped around each sword. The memorial was dedicated March, 1927.

The day I visited the Kyneton war memorial was chilly. Wrapping my scarf closer to my shoulders, I realized I was the only person in the park or viewing the memorial, which isn't unusual. Rarely are people around the war memorials unless there are benches. But as I stood there alone, under the huge trees, examining the many names listed on each side of the obelisk and imagining what those young men had endured, I felt very sad. Will my grandchildren's names one day be carved into a similar stone memorial? Or will we elect leaders who will lead toward understanding rather than battle?

Lancefield

For years I'd been blowing thank-you kisses from my kitchen windows to the young WWI French soldier standing quietly in the park across from my house in France. In late 1997 we moved from Hong Kong to Melbourne. We also bought a farm about an hour from Melbourne near a small town called Lancefield. We dreamed of an olive grove on the rolling hills and eventually planted 10,000 olive trees, which thrived in the rich soil of central Victoria.

One day while doing errands in Lancefield, I noticed a war memorial in the park. Over the years I'd become fairly good at spotting memorials in France and the habit continued. I was excited to see it and immediately went for a good look. The similarities between the soldiers from Montpezat and Lancefield were remarkable. Both young men have calm expressions, but the French soldier looks stoically ahead, while the Australian soldier gazes pensively downward as if remembering the battlefield's horror. Each man holds his rifle in front of his body. The hat is the only major difference. The Australian wears a floppy wide-brimmed hat cocked to one side; the French soldier wears a helmet. As I counted the names etched on the statue's base, I was surprised that each town, one in southwest France and one in rural Victoria, lost nearly the same number of men.

Australia lost more men per capita than any other country fighting in WWI, and all were volunteers. These men, many teenagers, lie beside men from other countries in the battlefields of Flanders, Somme, Ypres, Gallipoli, Verdun, Meuse-Argonne, and Marne. But none lie so far from home as do the Australian soldiers. Today French farmers dig up Australian belts, buckles, and ID tags while plowing their fields. Sometimes the Australian families are able to travel to France to retrieve the items and see where their loved one fell. This brings a closure to their mourning. Contemplating those thoughts, I decided to photograph Australian war memorials and combine them with my French photos. This would be my small endeavor to share with my family the horror of war. My idea was undeveloped, but I knew the finished task would not glorify war. Nor would I preach. Instead, I hoped showing the consequences of war from villages in France and Australia would be more powerful than my voice.

Mannum

Mannum has the reputation for having more fallen soldiers per capita in both World Wars than any other town in South Australia. Wendy Joseph wrote a song called "Year of the Drum," which describes the sorrow of wars for several generations of the people of Mannum.

The Mannum of today is a thriving town and popular tourist destination in the summer. Water skiing and wake-boarding are popular during the January holiday season. I thought it would be great fun to rent one of the house boats and float up and down the Murray River.

The day I visited the war memorial the bronze statue stood out against the bright blue sky and large billowing clouds. The soldier holds a rifle at the on-guard position and sits on a tall granite pedestal and plinth. It was difficult to see his face because of the sun, and as a result, I didn't experience the usual sorrow when viewing a monument. Perhaps it was the sun or because this soldier was in a ready-to-fight rather a contemplative position. Three steps made of the same granite and a concrete base anchor the memorial. A curved granite wall stands behind the memorial.

The plaque "Australia Remembers" is in the front of the memorial and behind is another plaque honoring the 50th anniversary of the landing of Gallipoli. It was unveiled by the governor in March, 1924, in front of about 1,000 persons. It lists the 37 people lost in the war. It cost 650 pounds. To the side is a German field gun presented to the town as a war trophy.

WWI 37 killed
2 named Tucker
2 named Read
2 named Rathmann
WWII 22 killed

Maryborough

The war memorial in the center of town was erected by the Women's Patriotic League. Many mothers, wives, sisters, aunts, and grandmothers in Australia became impatient with the slow political negotiations regarding the establishment of war memorials. They wanted to honor those who fell in the war immediately. In true practical and pioneer spirit they raised money and set in motion the steps necessary to create memorials suitable for their loved ones. In larger Australian towns there are often two war memorials, one established by a women's league and one by the government.

The Women's Patriotic League selected Margaret Baskerville as the designer for their war monument. It has a cast bronze soldier, standing on top of a stone pillar. The designer said, "He gazes at the enemy as he loads his gun, but his face is sad. The Australian soldier is not a man fond of taking life, but he had his duty to perform. That is what I have tried to portray in his face."

In addition to this grand bronze memorial I discovered six large grey granite pillars supporting the gateway to the city park. Some people wanted war memorials to be practical, such as a gate, a drinking fountain, a sports field, or school. Perhaps that was the thinking behind the beautifully built granite pillars supporting the wrought-iron gate. I like to think that whenever visitors to the park pass through the gates they are reminded of the men and woman who are buried far away from Australia.

WWI 309 soldiers killed				
5 nurses killed	2 Collett	4 Fisher	2 Holmes	3 Lee
2 Allen	2 Colman	2 Ford	2 Hopper	2 Liston
2 Ash	2 Cornwill	2 Garde	4 Hubble	2 Living
3 Blackway	2 Cox	2 Greenwood	2 Hughes	2 Llewellyn
6 Bartlett	2 Davidson	2 Greenwell	2 Humphries	2 Lord
2 Beasy	5 Davies	2 Grigg	2 Hyde	2 Lowday
3 Bell	2 Davis	3 Hall	3 James	2 Lunn
2 Bishop	2 Deady	2 Hare	4 Johnson	2 White
2 Blackburn	2 Diamond	2 Harrington	2 Jukes	2 Whiteley
3 Boyle	2 Dole	3 Harris	2 Judd	3 Wigger
2 Brangh	2 Buncombe	2 Hart	4 Jones	2 Williams
2 Brockwell	2 Eastman	3 Herring	2 Kerr	6 Wilson
6 Brown	5 Elliott	4 Higgens	2 Kofoed	2 Worsley
2 Chisholm	2 Emery	8 Hill	2 Ladd	2 Youlden
2 Christie	2 Hennessy	3 Holland	2 Layton	2 Zampatti

MADDER B.	MOWATT J.
*MAGUIRE J. T.	MOWATT W.
MANTON A.	MUIR S. V.
MANTON D. A.	MURFITT H.
MANTON H.	NESBITT A.
MARETT H. W.	NESBITT J.
MARETT A. T.	NEVILLE W. L.
MARSHALL W.	NICHOLLS J. T.
MARSHALL J. T.	NIGHTINGALE D.S.
MARTIN J. L.	NIGHTINGALE J. H.
MASON F. R.	NUNN E. L.
MATHERS W.R.H.	NUNN N. B.
MATTHEWS W. J.	OPEY J. T.
*MAYES G. E.	OSMOND W.
McALLESTER L.	*OSBORNE F.B.
McCANN A.	O'SULLIVAN D.
*McCANN G. E.	OWENS P.
McDONALD G.	*PALMER N. W.
McDONALD H.	PALMER W. E.
*McDONALD J. H.	PARKER R.
McKENZIE J.M.	PARKINSON S.
*McKELVIE A.	PASCOE J. R.
McLAY F.	PEARCE J. P.
McLEOD C.	PENROSE C. B.
MEANEY D.	*PERRATON H.
MELEN C.	PHILLIPS H. J.
MELLOW J. H.	POLLARD S. F.
*NEW B. A.	POLLOCK R.
NEW T. J.	PRICE A.
MILLER F. J. B.	*PRICE D. R.
MINAHAN E.	*PRICE J. O.
MINAHAN J.	PRICE L.
MINTER H. W	PRICE W. F.
MITCHELL E.	PURCELL H.
MITCHELL J.A.G.	PURCELL P. G.
*MITCHELL W.H.	*PURCELL W.
MOLE J.	*QUICK A.
MOLE W. J.	QUICK C.
MOON L. N.	QUICK R.
MOORE W.	RAITY C. H.
MORAN W. P.	*RANDALL F.
*MORRIS A.	RANKIN F. C.
MORRISON W.	RANKIN F. V.
MOSS C. H.	RANKIN J.
*MOSS W. K.	RANKIN W.
*MOTTRAM H.	*REYNOLDS
MOWATT C.	*READREAD

Terrible Human Losses for France

The French lost 1,383,000 soldiers from a total of 8,410,000 troops, an average of 900 killed every day.

Loss of officers was 18.9 percent.

Loss of troops was 16.1 percent.

The number of wounded is estimated at 3,594,900.

The number of mutilated or amputated at 100,000.

The number of blind or one-eye at 42,000.

Sixty percent had been hit by shrapnel, 34 percent by bullets, and 0.3 percent by knife.

In 2017, the latest figures estimate more French civilians than soldiers died.

Over 4,500 km of forest land was destroyed.

Over 21,000 km of farm land was ravaged.

Over 800,000 houses were ruined.

The Battle of Verdun

The Battle of Verdun in early 1916 was among the deadliest of the war. The Germans planned a slow-motion siege designed to drain French morale. The Germans brought 1,000 trains carrying shells for the attack. Three hundred thousand troops were in place and 165 airplanes would control the sky.

The German guns blasted French lines for hours, reducing them to mud and mulch. After three horrific days of bombardment, the French positions began to collapse. French General Petain arrived and kept open the 40-mile road that allowed taxis carrying soldiers and trucks with supplies to reach the front. Now this road is called the Sacred Way. But the battle became another stalemate and death-trap of the war. Both sides were bleeding and neither could give up. French Captain Desazneaux wrote, "It's a void. We are no longer in a civilized world. One suffers and says nothing."

Mildura

The land along the Murray River is flat, fertile, and irrigated with river water. The area supplies 80% of Victoria's grapes and a large percentage of citrus fruits and almonds. Many refer to Mildura as "Victoria's Food Bowl." Likewise, southwest France is called the "food basket of France." Another similarity between the two countries' towns represented in this book.

Mildura's war memorial is unique because it features a woman leaning against a white cross on top of a granite pedestal. It shows another comparison between French and Australian WWI war memorials. Many French war memorials show women figures, often as Marianne, the mother of France, or as mourning women of fallen sons, brothers, husbands, fathers, uncles and even grandfathers. The female figure reflects the aftermath of war and how women must rally their sorrow and get on with the job of gluing the broken pieces together. Very few Australian WWI monuments feature a woman or child, whereas many dramatic scenes of women, children, and the elderly are on French World War I monuments.

The Mildura monument is sometimes called the "Nurse Edith Cavell" monument, but there is no official reference to her. This description may have come about because at the time of the unveiling, Nurse Edith Cavell was executed by the Germans in 1915 for helping British, French, and Belgium soldiers during World War I. Many memorials to her memory were erected around the Commonwealth. To me this figure depicts womanhood and the myriad of emotional aspects she must feel at the loss of a loved one. She shows devotion, love, compassion, sorrow, helplessness, mercy, disgust, fear, exhaustion and loneliness. No names are listed.

There are many war monuments in the Mildura area. You can take a paddleboat on the Murray River War Trail and see a vast range of monuments in Victoria and South Australia. The goal is to "educate those traveling on our great river region to connect with the stories of those communities who acknowledge their fallen and showcase numerous museums, monuments, that preserve and protect the legacy of our diggers for the future." You can also see a descendent of the famous Lone Pine Hill tree. Two thousand men lost their lives in three days fighting on Lone Pine Hill in the middle east. A young Australian soldier at Gallipoli sent home pine seeds from the original lone pine tree in Gallipoli. After thirteen years the trees matured and were placed at Australian war memorials.

Mount Gambier

On October 1, 1922, the World War I memorial in Mount Gambier was dedicated in the city park. The entrance gate has two tall stone pillars and a wrought iron gate with large gold words reading LEST WE FORGET. The gate is very attractive and dramatically informs the visitor there will be a war memorial in this park. The impressive and tall war memorial sits on three block steps representing GOD, KING, COUNTRY. The four pillars signify RIGHTEOUSNESS, JUSTICE, FREEDOM AND PEACE. The canopy shows the emblem of the A.I.F. which is the rising sun. It expresses the determination of Australia to maintain the four principles on the pillars. The GLOBE represents the world and the CROSS is the symbol of sacrifice.

Many Australian memorials list the names of all those who served their country, not just those who fell. The park grounds have large palm, gum, cypress trees and rose gardens with decorative seasonal flowers surrounding the monument. In the distance is an elegant and well-maintained bandstand with a typical red tin roof and a cupola. It is surrounded by a Victorian wrought-iron fence and the red floor matches the roof. The foundation stone was laid in March 13, 1912, by C. McDonald Mayor of Mount Gambier.

Inside the bandstand is a war trophy of a 1917 Krupp Field Gun Model FK16 that was used by the German Imperial forces against the Allies during the war. The gun was captured on August 8, 1918, by soldiers of the 27th Battalion A.E.F. during action at Warfusee, Abancourt, in France. The gun was initially presented to the City of Adelaide, who in turn presented it to the town of Mount Gambier in 1920.

WWI 162 served/killed
WWII 58 served/killed

169

Murray Bridge

Like Mildura, Murray Bridge & District offers many water activities including house boats, paddle-steamers and beaches for relaxation and enjoying nature's beauty. You can take a safari bus with a personal guide to see the animals. Before the arrival of the Europeans, the area was inhabited by the Ngarrindjeri Aborigines. The river provided abundant fish, as well as good hunting grounds for kangaroos, emus, wombats, goannas, lizards, ducks, snakes, and bird eggs.

The World War I memorial was recently relocated to Bridge Street Park. In the background of the picture you'll see the large black granite obelisk with the names of the fallen soldiers. But the war trophy takes center stage. I want to point out again how much the Australian and French soldiers relied upon one another. This trophy was captured by South Australian's 10th Battalion near Haute Gruyere Farm, between Filleter and Bellicourt, on the Hindenburg Line on September 18, 1918. The plaque reads:

THIS GERMAN FIELD GUN, A SOUVENIR OF THE GREAT WAR 1914–18
WAS PRESENTED TO THE CITY OF MURRAY BRIDGE & DISTRICT
IN RECOGNITION OF THOSE WHO SERVED.

Considering how many dead Australian soldiers were buried in France, these guns very likely killed soldiers from South Australia. As a result, they were usually welcomed as traditional trophies and usually set beside the local WWI memorials. About 500 artillery pieces, 400 trench mortars, and 4,000 machine guns were sent to Australia, and many remain alongside the memorials. People had two very different perceptions of these "gifts." Some were insulted by the offer of a mere machine gun when they wanted a mortar. Others refused any instruments of war, saying having them at the memorial site gave a message of militarism. I tend to agree with the latter, but as modern war killing is increasingly done via drones managed by soldiers in offices far from the war zone, I'm beginning to think that these war trophies might be good reminders to our youth that, after all, war remains a form of destruction.

Murtoa

A quiet and peaceful town, Murtoa sits in the wheat district near Lake Marma and 190 miles northwest of Melbourne. McDonald is the main street of Murtoa and is flanked by fine old trees and 1910-era buildings with timber facades and verandah posts. The war memorial is located on Lake street and commemorates the residents of Murtoa who died in World War I, World War II, and the Vietnam War.

The only word to describe this war memorial is grand. It consists of a set of large brilliant white gates and two wrought-iron fences and a continuing low white fence. A WWI soldier stands at attention on the top of the gate's curved arch. On one side of the arch is a grey granite sign:

MURTOA'S TRIBUTE 1920

On the other side is a matching granite sign:

THE GREAT WAR 1914–1919

Four pillars reinforce the overall structure. The innermost pillars each have a gray granite sign, listing those who died in service, nine names on one and ten on the other. Four plaques on the remaining pillars list the 100 names of the returned soldiers. Behind the lower walls are eight tall cedar trees and two flag poles with Australian flags flying high.

This Murtoa memorial is splendid. It invites you into a large generous park. It remembers both the fallen and returned soldiers. The large native gum trees rise high into the bright blue Australian sky with white billowing clouds. I wanted to pause, take some deep breaths, and thank those who built this fine memorial. My spirits were lifted.

WWI
19 killed
100 returned

Port Fairy

Port Fairy is a pretty, small, freshly washed coastal town and port in SW Victoria 180 miles west of Melbourne where the Moyne River enters the Southern Ocean. It is one of my favorite Australian towns and recently discovered while driving my French friends along the Great Ocean Road. We stayed overnight in Port Fairy and were tired after a long drive. After dinner there wasn't enough energy to walk around the town and we retired early. When the bright sunny morning arrived, we were delighted to see sparkling water and a charming main street and to learn there were 50 buildings protected by the National Trust of Australia. There are bluestone buildings, white-washed whaler's cabins, Georgian-style merchant's homes and you can visit the Maritime Shipwreck Heritage Walk and light house.

In a small park on Bank Street stands the simple yet proud World War I memorial. It has two linked chain fences surrounding it, probably because the road runs nearby. At the top of the obelisk a lone soldier stands at attention with his right hand on the rifle barrel and his Australian hat cocked to the right side of his head.

Red stone plaques are placed on each side of the memorial base, listing the names of the soldiers who fought and died in both world wars. By this time I was getting used to the long lists of names on Australian memorials, but my French guests, who often helped me find French war memorials, were extremely surprised to see how many young men fought in the Great War. They would shake their heads in disbelief while counting the names. Looking at me for explanation they'd ask, "Why were so many Australians sent to France? Where are they buried?" When I replied, "They volunteered to serve their King and they are buried in France," they would look at each other, sometimes touch tenderly the engraved names, and then look down or in the distance. We went to the harbor for a simple lunch and watched the many boats and birds, but we didn't talk much. We were processing the deep unanswerable questions of war.

WWI
129 names
WWII
13 names

Portland

Portland is the oldest city in the state of Victoria and sits beside Portland Bay. James Grant named the bay Portland when he sailed in the Lady Nelson in 1800. It is the only deep sea port between Adelaide and Melbourne and offers a sheltered home from the often very fierce weather of Bass Strait.

The Gunditjmara people still live around the district and are considered very important in scientific circles for their early aquaculture development near Lake Condah. The Gunditjmara made settlements and lived in small circular stone huts. Archeological digs have found the Gunditjmara ancestors also lived in villages of weather-proof houses with stone walls a meter high, around eel traps and aquaculture ponds. On just one hectare of Allambie Farm, archeologists discovered 160 house sites.

Two tourist draws are the 250-km walking track called the Great South West Walk and the Portland Maritime Museum. Koalas, seals, and whales are regular visitors to Portland. Koalas can often be found in city parks, seals often visit the city boat ramp, and southern right whales and humpbacks enter the bay annually.

We didn't spend much time in Portland after our lazy morning in Port Fairy. Fortunately, I found one of the eight memorials now listed on Wikipedia. It is situated in a large park surrounded by fine bluestone buildings, rose beds, and walkways. A soldier stands atop a red stone pedestal shaped like a temple. He is looking down and holding his rifle in front of his legs. Once again his head is covered by the wide-brimmed Australian hat cocked to the right side.

Sadly, I didn't write the number of names on the memorial, but the photo clearly shows many names.

Portland Cement Company Ltd.

This memorial stands tall on Ocean Blvd. and Scholefield Road in Seacliff, S.A., a suburb of Portland. The South Australian Portland Cement Company war memorial was built for the employees of the company who served in World War I. It is a rendered cement column on a two-stepped brick base. On the top you see rifles with bayonets extended pointing toward the sky. It is a clean and simple memorial but speaks a strong message. This company appreciated their employees.

This is another example of wide diversity of war memorials in Australia. About 35,000 South Australian served in the First World War. That was 8.5% of the South Australian population at the time, or 37.7% of the men between the ages of 18 and 44! Of those who served, over 5,000 South Australians died.

Some say this war touched every Australian heart in one way or another. If you didn't lose a family member, it could be a work colleague, friend, doctor, pastor, neighbor's son, and on and on. This war was similar to dropping a boulder in a puddle.

Red Cliffs

Red Cliffs is important to the subject of this book because in 1918 the Australian government opened the area to 770 ex-service men under the Soldier Settlement Scheme. These soldiers became diligent settlers in very harsh environmental conditions during the stressful times and uncertainty of worldwide economic forces. Their hard work was fundamental to the establishment of the vineyards, which have become the town's chief industry. It was such a successful program that after World War II, the Australian government sold land to new veterans who wanted to settle in Red Cliffs.

Sitting on display near the World War Monument is the permanent display of Big Lizzie, a large tractor built by F. Bottrill, the designer, builder and operator of the machine. Bovril was inspired by his experiences in the 1880s while watching the suffering of camels carrying heavy loads. It was so slow it took over two years (1917–1919) to travel from Melbourne to the Red Cliffs. The turning circle took 200-feet radius to turn around. It towed two enormous trailers, each with their own water and oil reserve tanks and an overall carrying capacity of 80 tons. The wheels are designed to work in sandy soils and for five years it cleared mallee scrub around Red Cliffs area then moved to Glen dinning Station near Balmoral. It continued to work for 40 years but eventually was replaced by the caterpillar track. When Big Lizzie was built, it was the biggest tractor in Australia and thought to be the biggest in the world.

The Red Cliffs memorial is powerful without being ostentatious. It is modern and located in a large park with mature native and non-native trees. A large paved path leads to the memorial highlighting a medium sized white obelisk. On either side of the obelisk two red brick walls display black plaques listing the names of soldiers from each war. There are three white flag poles to one side of the memorial, but the flags were not flying on the day I visited the site. The park is spacious and I felt calm. A soft breeze ruffled my hair while I read the long list of names. Slowly my mind pictured battles and soldiers' descriptions of battles filled my mind—I felt grateful for this peaceful park. Maybe it will be an ideal antidote to the ugly experiences these young men endured during the wars and a solace for the loved one's families left behind. War doesn't end with the death of a soldier. The ripples go on and on through generations.

Robe

Robe is one of the oldest towns in South Australia, founded as a seaport and village before the Province of South Australia was established. During the gold rush period around 1857, over 16,000 Chinese people landed at Robe to travel overland to the goldfields. The state of Victoria introduced a 10-pound landing tax on each person as one way of reducing the number of Chinese immigrants. After making their way across the long ocean trip to Australia from China, getting through customs, and paying the tax, they still had to walk the 200 miles to Ballarat and Bendigo.

With the advent of railways Robe's importance waned, but it has remained a local service center for the surrounding rural areas. A fleet of fishing boats call Robe their home, especially those who fish for the delicious local lobsters.

The lone rank and file soldier stands upon a five-tiered monument. He could be one of the 250 statues of a digger standing on similar Australian war memorials. The statues were created in the 1920s and often not made by Australian sculptors or even made in Australia. A great many were imported ready-carved from the workshops in Italy.

Underneath the block on which the soldier stands is a carved wreath. The bottom step is dedicated to those who lost their lives in the Second World War. The backdrop for the Robe memorial is a large bushy palm tree and in the distance other taller trees frame the statue. This photo was taken as the sun was setting and I was happy to have enough light to capture the scene. These lone soldiers, so familiar in style to the soldier near my French house, pull my heart strings. They look lonely standing in quiet spaces without any one around.

WWI 14 killed
WWII 8 killed

Romsey

Prior to the European settlement, Romsey was inhabited by aborigines from the Wurundjeri tribe. They were nomadic but had tribal rights to occupy and use tracts of land for gathering seeds and roots, fishing the streams and camping. Those who lived near Romsey were the Kurrajeberring clan and in 1830 it was estimated that between forty and sixty per cent of Victorian aborigines died in a smallpox epidemic before 1835. Nearly ninety percent succumbed to European diseases and viral infections.

Edward Dryden wrote: "In 1839 I took possession of the Mt. Macedon Station which I have occupied until the present hour, depasturing sheep and cattle. Of the aborigines at my time of locating there, there was one tribe consisting of about 150, including adult males, females and children of both sexes who camped in their mia-mias. They were exceedingly simple in their manner and perfectly harmless in their bearing. I never heard of a single outrage committed by anyone of them by any settler."

Through the years, research at nearby Mt. William has revealed that the axe quarry played a major role in the social and economic life of aborigines. The Wurundjeris made and bartered the highly prized tools. Another scared site of the Wurundjeris is the burial cave in a gorge at Springfield, where a 17-year-old girl was buried about three hundred years ago. With her remains were decorated possum skins, a woven netting bag, bundles of emu feathers, shaped emu bones, and stone artifacts.

Romsey's war memorial sits along the Lancefield-Melbourne highway south of town. While the war raged overseas, many of the wounded servicemen were brought to Romsey from crowded Melbourne hospitals. The memorial is another typical Australian soldier standing on a pedestal. He stares ahead, a carved tree trunk is at his side, and he holds a rifle with both hands. The same Australian wide-brimmed hat sits on his head. On Anzac and Remembrance days the Romsey residents place small white crosses at the foot of the statue. Sometimes they have the traditional red poppy and other times a small Australian flag attached. There is street light near the statue that lights his figure at night. I like that feature.

Rushworth

Rushworth is a small town in the state of Victory about 98 miles north of Melbourne. At the 2011 census it had a population of 1,381. It was established during the gold rush in 1853 and named by a poet and later local Goldfields Commissioner Richard H. Horne in 1854. A common explanation for how it was named is that Horne met too good friends on the trip to Australia. One was named Rush and the other More. He honored them by naming the new town Rushmore. Its post office was opened in 1857.

Rushworth is a sleepy town with a nice wide park through the center of town, large natural gum trees, and pleasant traditional and modern homes. There were a few stores, but it wasn't a busy town when I visited it at least fifteen years ago.

The war memorial I found in Rushworth is unique. Rather than a statue or obelisk, it has a wall plaque inside a covered sitting area in the middle of the park. Inside is a long wooden bench and the day I took the photo shown here simple bouquets of flowers were resting on the bench, presumably honoring the fallen soldiers. This simple resting place is made even more special by the tower on the roof with a handsome black and white clock.

St. Arnaud

St. Arnaud is located in the Wimmera region of Victoria. There are elegant private homes with attractive gardens as well as public gardens in St. Arnaud's town center. Queen Mary Gardens has a large pond and a generous selection of trees from other lands, all linked together with graceful paths, benches, and picnic tables. Pioneer Park and Lord Nelson Park have a good selection of sporting and recreational facilities. You can visit one of the town's last mines at a lookout on Wilson Hill, which has a honeycomb of mine shafts.

The streets downtown in St. Arnaud are wide and lined with leafy trees. I wanted to stay longer in this gracious town with so many beautifully maintained buildings and peaceful parks. It was gracious and calm.

The elegant brick-and-plaster town hall facade is the war memorial in St. Arnaud. It appears that the town hall porch was added to the building to commemorate the soldiers who served in World War I. Two statues are placed in niches on each side of the balcony and they resemble other Australian WWI statues. They gaze calmly ahead and hold their rifles with both hands. Below each statue, but on the first floor level, are two blue gray stone tablets edged in black and a wreath on top. They list the names of those who fell during the war or died of wounds after the war. To the best of my ability I counted 24 names.

Before I continued my travel toward another war memorial, I paused to admire the creativity of St. Arnaud war memorial. Standing there, I pondered how long it took the citizens and politicians to decide on this magnificent memorial. It was a good decision.

Tanunda

In 1843 a second group of German immigrants established a small settlement on the banks of the North Para River. It was named Langmeil (Long Mile). The first German settlement came in 1842 and was named Behaneen. During the Great War Langmeil and Behaneen were renamed Bilyara and Bethany due to prejudicial worries about German settlers. In Australia there were about 100,000 Germans in 1914 and during WWI it was a very difficult time for German-Australians. Before the war the Germans were respected and made major contributions, especially in South Australia, where nearly 10% of the population was of German heritage. But when Germany became the enemy, anti-German fear grew. However, the Germans were politically, with a few exceptions, loyal to Australia. Many German-Australians fought in the Australian army and died for Australia. In fact, General John Monash was Australia's most famous commander in the war. He was the son of German-Jewish immigrants and was fluent in German. After the war many Australians did not want statues of General Monash because of his heritage. Fortunately, those feelings changed and now the prestigious Monash University in Melbourne leads international research across many academic disciplines.

Langmeil had its name reverted from Bilyara in 1975. Eventually, the villages of Langmeil and Tanunda were joined together into the township of Tanunda, an Aboriginal word meaning "water hole."

In the Garden of Remembrance a white marble "Cross of Remembrance" sits on a marble pedestal and base, a humble memorial erected by the Tanunda Women's Organization. The garden is calm. I remained there a long time thinking about Australia's German immigrants. The thoughts brought home my childhood memories of my German father in the United States and his entire family in Germany. I grew up with WWII and believed the propaganda about evil Germans. Hitler's actions were evil, but I was conflicted. My father was loving and kind and my grandmother, aunts, uncles, and cousins lived in Hamburg, where heavy bombing occurred. I had to come to terms with the complexities of who is "bad" and who is "good." This little war memorial in Tanundra reaffirmed the lessons my mother and father taught me: behaviors determine good and bad, not nations.

Tooborac

Tooborac is a rural town established in a district primarily used for grazing sheep. It is on the Northern Highway nine miles southeast of Heathcote. Its name might be an Aboriginal word describing a local hill. As I travelled through Tooborac, the surroundings looked bleak and dry. The sky was covered with heavy dark clouds and there were acres of untended dry fields. However the Tooborac Hotel caught my attention. It is a nice bluestone building with a front bar and open fireplaces, but I didn't sample the food.

For such a small town I was surprised to find a very tall and powerful war memorial. It is weather-worn and in need of care but continues to emit great authority and dignity. The soldier stands on a series of eleven large block steps. He is so high up you must lift your head to see his somber face. He stands at attention with his rifle at his right side and his left hand against his hip. He definitely gives the feeling he is a man of action. His Australian wide-brimmed hat with one side cocked softens his demeanor.

The eleven steps are surrounded by a black linked chain fence attached to the four outside corner rough stone pillars. At least ten bouquets of flowers were randomly placed on the steps.

The sun began to glow through the clouds when I took the photo, giving a dramatic mood. Sadly the names were beyond readability. Eighteen names might be a good guess. World War II soldiers were not listed, but a plaque commemorated them.

The war memorial is a tribute to how much these young men were loved and missed by their families and friends. I felt gratitude and humility looking at the statue and thinking about the hard-working and loyal people who lost their loved ones.

Warracknabeal

Warracknabeal is a rural town in the state of Victoria, situated on the banks of the Yarriambiack Creek, about 220 miles north-west of Melbourne. The Aboriginal people who lived around Warracknabeal belonged to the Wotjobaluk tribe. The name of the town probably came from an expression meaning "place of big gums shading the water." There are several impressive historical buildings in the town. The accompanying photo shows the 1907 red brick and half-timber two-story Tudor style building near the World War I memorial. You will be charmed by the sculpture of full-sized sheep and a kelpie dog placed in the middle of a roundabout. It honors the town's early days.

The attractive Yarriambiack Creek runs through the town and is lined with river gums and home to many water birds. There are several parks and gardens along both sides of the creek, and foot bridges allow you to frequently cross the creek.

The war memorial stands on three rough-cut stone steps. The pillar section is made of carved and smoothed stone. The traditional Australian soldier stands on top of the pedestal. He wears the standard cocked hat and stares calmly into the distance while holding the angled rifle in both hands. These subtle differences between quite similar statues intrigue me.

The carved black words say:

FOR KING AND COUNTRY.
A GRATEFUL TRIBUTE TO THE MEN OF THE SHIRE OF BORUNG WHO MADE
THE SUPREME SACRIFICE IN THE GREAT WAR 1914-1919.
"THEIR NAMES SHALL LIVE FOREVER."

Warrnambool

Warrnambool is a popular tourist stop with nearly one million persons visiting each year. Views from the Great Ocean Road, sighting of whales, camping, two children's festivals, and surfing are some of the many activities around Warrnambool.

It was a great surprise to come across the enormous WWI war memorial in Warrnambool. It has a large curved brick wall with twelve deep brown plaques listing the names of soldiers. Each plaque has approximately 82 names, or nearly 1,000 names, carved into the memorial walls. In front of the wall is a very tall pillar and on top is a golden angel with spreading wings. Below is a temple shaped structure with the traditional Australian soldier facing forward as if remembering the horror of war. He wears the Australian uniform, with Australian hat, and his hands hold the rifle in front of this legs. In another photo from Wikipedia I noted that the rifle had been removed.

It was a blustery cold day when I visited the memorial. I wasn't dressed warmly, so I hurried back to the warm car and missed an opportunity to photographs more details. Regardless of the weather, I was deeply impressed with this elaborate and luxurious war memorial. Its size, the quality of the material, the site, the wide green surroundings, and richly planted flowers beds all give a grandiose feeling without pretentiousness. I longed for a warm day when I could spend hours wandering around the memorial, reading the many names and allowing myself to once again reflect on the consequences of war.

In our modern busy world, where new technology has invaded our lives under the guise of making lives easier, I often think it has added more clutter and distraction for me. Perhaps it is my age, or that I don't take time to pause, but by visiting a war memorial I slow down temporarily and focus on the moment while contemplating the bigger questions of life. Visiting war memorials might be an excellent way for everyone to learn about our history, calm down, and connect with issues larger than what we've written on the daily "to do" list. Not only do I thank the men and woman who are named on the memorials but also the women and men who built and maintain these grand and humble spaces.

LOONEY J.	MILES L.
LOUEZ A.	MILES W.
LOUGHEED P.	MILLER J.
LOVEKIN F.	MILLER W.
LOVEKIN G.K.	MILLER W.
LOVELL C.H.	MILLIKEN E.
LOW J.S.	MILNE A.D.
LUDEMAN E.	MILNE G.
LUKER A.R.	MILNE J.W.
LUKER P.	MITCHELL A.
LYNCH J.	MITCHELL A.
MACHAREY E.	MITCHELL D.
MACKAY D.C.	MITCHELL J.A.
MACKNIGHT C.C.	MITCHELL J.
MacLAREN L.	MITCHELL S.
MACONACHIE W.	MITCHELL W.
MAHONEY W.J.	MOLESWORTH W.F.
MAINLAND D.	MONTGOMERY G.A.
MAKIN F.H.	MOORE C.
MALONEY H.	MORGAN D.
MALONEY R.S.	MORGAN S.
M°KINLAY S.	MORTON J.F.
MANSBRIDGE B.	MORETON R.A.
MANSELL G.	MORETON S.
MANSELL H.	MORETON V.
MANSON H.A.	MORETON W.
MARFELL W.L.	MORSE H.D.
MARKS T.A.	MUNRO R.W.
MATHIESON C.B.	MURIEL A.R.
MATTHEW N.J.	MURNANE A.
MATTINSON W.H.	MURPHY S.
MAULDON J.	MURRAY J.
MAYNARD H.W.	McBRIDE G.
MEAD E.	McCALLUM D.
MEE D.W.	McCALLUM M.
MELKCOMS A.	McCARTHY F.J.
MELVILLE L.	McCARTHY J.
MEMBRY C.H.	McCONNELL J.F.
MEMBRY T.	McCLURE H.
MEWHA H.	McCULLOUGH J.
MEWHA J.	McDONALD D.

Cooper

Walking quietly through the German cemetery in Belgium, my grandson Shata Liam tapped my shoulder and motioned me to follow him to a grave. We paused in respect and shock. Buried here was a 14-year-old boy. Shata Liam put his arm around my shoulder and said, "He was younger than me." We hugged with tears in our eyes.

My Final Thoughts

Thank you for joining me on a twenty-five-year journey to better understand World War I. Even though I was often sad when pausing before each memorial in France and Australia, I was rewarded by increased admiration for those who fought and died and how their families honored them.

After visiting over 1,500 war memorials, I could not identify positive aspects to WWI until I read *To End All Wars*, by Adam Hochschild. He opened my eyes to small and larger ways the war slowly moved humanity toward human equality and my thoughts here are inspired by his book. More than a million men from British colonies fought for the empire in World War I. Slowly these soldiers began to see themselves in a new light. The same is true with the Indian troops. They wrote home telling their families that British nurses emptied their bedpans, tidied their beds, fed them, and offered genuine compassion. The war awoke the identities of British colonies. White colonists were affected too. The horrendous loss of men and the bitterness combined with war memories of Australian and Canadian soldiers sacrificed at Passchendaele and Gallipoli by inept British generals simmered during the war's aftermath. British West Indian soldiers mutinied when they were commanded to clean white soldiers' toilets and failed to get a pay increase the whites had received. One officer wrote, "Nothing we can do will alter the fact that the black man has begun to think and feel himself as good as white." In Belize, capital of British Honduras, veterans rioted against their status as second-class citizens in their homeland.

The British empire slowly crumbled over the course of the century, Ireland being the first to begin guerilla warfare. Finally, ten years after WWI, the cavalry lance was retired as a combat weapon. Mussolini was rising in Italy. The foundation of apartheid was growing in South Africa. British military executions for military discipline were debated. Citizens asked counsel about war executions. Were executions to enforce military discipline or done by bullheaded generals who did not accept that trench warfare could drive men mad? People questioned whether desertion and casting away arms were done by tragic victims or by heroes refusing to continue in the madness of war.

Today I remain confused about the aftermath of the war. Was the enormous death toll necessary to prevent Germany controlling all of Europe? Or was it a senseless ego-filled endeavor that only made world cooperation more difficult? Many scholars advise us to study WWI before making judgements of WWII. My teenage German father was a WWI seaman, and when he returned home, he was determined to leave Germany. He said the German mood was already boiling for revenge, which helped the rise of Nazism.

WWI smashed many morals and the difference between soldiers and civilians was removed. Chemical warfare, the torpedoing of neutral ships, and blockades starving civilians became possible. Barbed-wire-ringed camps in Germany for laborers conscripted from France, Belgium, and Russia were repeated by Nazis and Soviets. The Turkish genocide of the Armenians would be repeated against Europe's Jews. Poison gas from American spraying of defoliants across South Vietnam increased the birth defects. The list of consequences of WWI is very long.

A thin line of land stretching through northern France and a corner of Belgium has the greatest concentration of young men's graves in the world. Miles of orderly thickets of white tombstones or crosses climb low hills, gentle valleys, sometimes with spires, columns, and rotundas. From the New Zealand memorial in Messines, Belgium, to the South African National Memorial at the Somme battlefield in France to the less grand cemeteries holding the bones of Senegalese troops or Chinese labors, the land reminds the viewer of how far men traveled to die. Even those lucky to be in marked graves were sometimes buried twice over—cemeteries from the first year or two of the war were blown up by shells in later battles. Today there are more than 2,000 British cemeteries alone in France and Belgium.

My grandsons and I were guided to a empty space in a French forest that was once a farm village. It was blown apart and toxins made it impossible for the villagers to rebuild their farms. Later we came to a quiet spot not far from a busy road where once enemy soldiers met at Christmas in 1914 to play soccer. Small white crosses were placed by a faded, fallen Christmas tree, reminding visitors to remember the moment of peace between enemies.

Hochschild noted, "Nowhere along the western front do you find a peacemaker's memorial." Why is that? I don't have an answer, but I hope someone younger and wiser than myself will wake up to the fact that 100 years after the war to end all wars we are still at war. My hope is that one day we will not only honor our countries but expand our vision to honor our world. Perhaps the battle for climate change will bring more cooperation between countries. We need fresh and compassionate persons waking us up to the many possibilities of working together.

Bibliography

Barnett, Correlli. *The Swordbearers: Supreme Command in the First World War*. Bloomington: Indiana University Press, 1963.

Benson, Sir Irving. *The Man with the Donkey*. London: Hodder & Stoughton, 1965.

Brocklehurst, Ruth, and Henry Brook. *The Usborne Introduction to the First World War*. Internet: Usborne-quicklinks.com.

Buffetant, Yves. *The Battle of Verdun*. France: Ysec Editions, 2018.

Calder, Angus, Ed. *Wars*. New York: Penguin Books, 1999.

Cole, Robert. *A Traveller's History of France, 3rd Edition*. UK: The Windrush Press.

De Schaepdrijver, Sophie, and Tammy M. Proctor. *An English Governess in the Great War*. Five bound diaries of Mary Thorp a governess in Brussels.

De Vries, Susanna. *Heroic Australian Women in War: Gallipoli to Kokada*. Sydney: Harper Collins, 2004.

Downing, W.H. To the Last Ridge: *The First World War Memories of W.H. Downing*. Australia: Duffy & Snellgrove, 1998. This book is compared to Erich Maria Remarque's All Quite on the Western Front. It describes Australian activities in France and where the dead rest.

Dyer, Geoff. *The Missing of the Somme*. New York: Vintage Books, 1994.

Englund, Peter. *The Beauty and the Sorrow: An Intimate History of the First World War*. New York: Alfred A. Knopf, 2011.

Farrar-Hockley, A.H. *The Somme*. London: Pan Books 1966.

Ferguson, Niall. *The Pity of War*. New York: Basic Books, 1999.

Gerike, Ann. *About/Face: World War I Facial Injury and Reconstruction*. Seattle: Floating Bridge Press, 2013.

Gibbs, Nancy. Ed. *The War That Shaped Our World*. New York: Time Inc. Books, 2017.

Helprin, Mark. *A Soldier of the Great War*. Orlando, FL: Harcourt Brace Jovanovich, 1991.

Hochschild, Adam. To *End All Wars: Loyalty and Rebellion 1914–1918*. New York: Harcourt, 2004.

Inglis, K.S. *Sacred Places: War Memorial in the Australian Landscape*. Melbourne: Melbourne University Press, 1998. This excellent and scholarly book about war memorials helped me set the framework for my study of WWI. Inglis began his survey of war memorials throughout Australia in 1983. It will help any reader understand the significance of WWI and WWII.

Laffin, John. *The Western Front Illustrated 1914–1918*. Sydney: Kangaroo Press, 1993.

Laffin, John. *Epitaphs of World War I: We Will Remember Them*. Sydney: Kangaroo Press, 1995.

Lewis, Jon E. Ed. *The Mammoth Book of War Diaries and Letters in the Words of Ordinary Soldiers*. London: Robinson, 1998.

Levy, Daniel S., Ed. *World War I: The Great War and the American Century*. New York: Life Books, 2017.

Masefield, John. *The Old Front Line*. United Kingdom: Pen & Sword Books, 2003.

Mead, Gary. *The Dough Boys: America in the First World War*. Woodstock, NY: Overlook Press, 2000.

Morgan, Brinley. *The Raglan Fallen: A Memorial to the Sons of Raglan Who Fell in the Great War 1914–1918*. 2016.

Murray, Williamson. *History of Warfare: War in the Air 1914–45*. London: Cassell, 1999.

Nicholls, R.A. *Timeline of War*. Canary Press, Barnes and Noble, 2008.

OREP tourist booklet. *World War I: From Mobilization to the Armistice*. Bayeux, France.

OREP tourist booklet. *The American Soldier*. Bayeux, France.

Palmer, Svetlana, and Sarah Wallis. *Intimate Voices from the First War*. New York: Harper Collins, 2003.

Pugsley, Christopher and John Lockyer. *The Anzacs at Gallipoli*. Auckland: Reed Children's Books, 1997.

Reifsnyder, Henry G. *A Second-Class Private in the Great War: Personal Diary of H.G. Reifsnyder 1917–19*. Printed for private distribution only. Philadelphia, 1923.

Remarque, Eric Maria. *All Quiet on the Western Front*. New York: Ballantine Books, 1958.

Steel, Nigel. *Gallipoli.* United Kingdom: Pen & Sword Books, 1999.

Strachan, Hew. *The First World War.* United Kingdom: Simon & Schuster, 2003. This book covers WWI in Africa, Indonesia, Japan, Rhodesia, German-Ottoman Alliance, Caucus, Armenia, Senegal, India, Algeria, Gallipoli, Mesopotamia, and East Prussia.

Walker, Martin. *The Dark Vineyard.* New York: Vintage Books, 2011.

Westwell, Ian. *World War I.* London: Hermes House, 2008. This book offers 500 excellent photos, a detailed timeline, and numerous maps.

...................., *Forward March.* Produced by the disabled American veterans of the world war department of rehabilitation. Printed in the USA, MCMXXXIV–V. My father, Eric A.A. Peters, owned this book. He served in the German merchant marine on the North Sea in WWI. Excellent photos and commentaries. Proceeds went to wounded veterans.

About the Author

Marie Peters has lived in eight countries on four continents: North America, Europe, Asia, and Australia. She began journaling nearly 40 years ago to record her experiences while abroad and the memories they evoked and as part of her continual search for authenticity.

This book about World War I memorials began 25 years ago when Marie lived in France and Australia. She compared WWI war memorials in both countries by taking photos and eventually decided to write this book in honor of all war victims and to alert her six grandchildren about the waste and horror of war.

Professionally, Marie has written educational articles and books related to students with special needs, their families, and adopting children of other races. She was married twice and adopted two children: a mixed-race daughter while living in Oregon and a Chinese son while living in Hong Kong.

Marie lives in the Mt. Baker neighborhood of Seattle, Washington, with her rescue dog and cat, Taz and Colette. She continues to write and sketch in her journals, paint her spirit sticks, and enjoy the company of friends and family, particularly her beloved teenage grandsons in Seattle and her granddaughter and three grandsons in Australia.